WHAT PEOPLE ARE SAYING
ABOUT *THE MAP* . . .

Effective leaders are grounded in their values and secure in who they are—a maturity not easily won and achieved by too few. In clear and compelling terms, *The Map* charts a tangible course for accelerating growth to become the kind of genuine leaders that our organizations, communities, families, and even the world urgently need.

John L. Thornton
Chairman, Barrick Gold Corporation
Chairman, The Brookings Institute and Former President of Goldman Sachs

The leaders who have changed the world have stood on their values. They have been shaped by the challenges they have faced more than the privileges of their upbringing. It is not an easy road, but it is an easy burden. *The Map* points us in the right direction.

Ambassador Andrew Young
Former Mayor of Atlanta and US Ambassador to the United Nations

Few books about leadership are as thoughtful and insightful as *The Map*. Using abundant examples and their own meticulous research, the authors give leaders at all levels a guide on how to lean into challenges and take control of their journeys to more effective leadership. They argue persuasively that everyone can get to "the Promised Land."

John E. Schlifske
Chairman and CEO, Northwestern Mutual

The Map provides a tectonic shift in our thinking about how leaders can be most effective in their roles. It takes us beyond knowledge and skills to show how our experiences can be a transformative crucible for the highest level of leadership.

Dale E. Jones
CEO, Diversified Search
Corporate Director, Kohls and Northwestern Mutual Life

I'm still journeying toward my Promise Land, and I am grateful to have Keith and Karl's "map" to guide me. Indeed, the map has been the one thing that has kept me from straying too far off course. Readers who genuinely want to grow will find Keith and Karl's insights invaluable professionally and personally. May the true journey, with all its highs and lows, now begin!

Stuart Gulley, PhD,
President, Woodward Academy
Author of *The Academic President as Moral Leader: James T. Laney at Emory University, 1977-1993*

This book is a must read. It provides fresh analytical insights and tools for aspiring and seasoned leaders who want to bring their inward and outward journey into greater focus. I can testify to its clarity and power! Supplemented by a one-on-one engagement with Dr. Eigel, these principles helped me discover the pathway to a much more developed version of myself, to the benefit of those in both my personal and professional life. I now have a deeper spiritual energy and a stronger psychological tendency to pause and step back from high-pressure situations, and, with better timing, re-enter the fray—ready, willing and able to add the highest value. That has made me a better leader and a better man!

Dr. John Sylvanus Wilson, Jr.
11th President of Morehouse College
Former Executive Director of The White House Initiative on Historically Black Colleges and Universities

Making our way through the journey of life is full of challenges. Eigel and Kuhnert have shown us how those challenges are actually the fuel for taking us further down our life's path. They have also shown that engaging this journey is the key to improving the quality and effectiveness of our leadership—in the broadest sense possible. To do this they have taken a very complex subject, human developmental growth, and conveyed the essential points with an elegant simplicity. The combination of ideas, stories and practices presented in *The Map* can aid anyone in the work of leading . . . in our own lives and in serving those around us.

Jonathan Reams, PhD
Associate Professor, Education and Lifelong Learning at The Norwegian University of Science and Technology
Editor in Chief, *Integral Review Journal*
Co-founder of The Center for Transformative Leadership and The European Center for Leadership Practice.

The Map brings the process of psychological growth to the center of leadership development. It is indeed challenging to be successful at leadership without psychological growth and development. As someone who has spent years studying the risks of narcissistic leadership, and someone who has had the good fortune of taking Keith and Karl's leadership training course, I strongly endorse their approach.

W. Keith Campbell, PhD
Co-author, *The Narcissism Epidemic: Living in the Age of Entitlement*

I have had the privilege of working with Dr. Eigel on this journey of growth at the University of West Georgia. Our "Engage West!" initiative of evidence-based leadership and a culture of high performance has at its core the belief that being engaged in growing ourselves will in fact grow others. The "map" described Eigel's and Kunhert's book is an invitation to a journey . . . a journey that has the power of transforming yourself, impacting the people around you and the organizations you lead.

Dr. Kyle Marrero
President, University of West Georgia

Karl and Keith have written a very engaging and insightful book on leadership. It is unlike most leadership books that attempt to take lessons from effective leaders and apply them to everyone in leadership roles. By and large those books attempt to distill a list of things that great leaders do into a shorter list of things that anyone can (or should be able to) do. Keith and Karl take a different approach: They correctly note that it is impossible to separate *what a leader does* from *who a leader is*. Leadership effectiveness occurs in the context of the maturity and experience of the leader. This book provides practical advice and coaching to guide the leader (or the aspiring leader) to grow from their personal challenges and obstacles. These are important leadership insights, whether you are leading your business, team, family, or social group.

Michael Jenkins, PhD
Senior Associate Director of Executive Programs
The Terry College of Business at the University of Georgia

This excellent book provides a compelling guide for achieving your potential as a leader. Unlike so many anecdotally driven leadership books, this guide is based on more than twenty years of research by two of the most original, insightful thought leaders in the field. They describe the complexities of leadership development as both Lateral (building new skill sets) and Vertical (learning new mindsets). The book delineates the path to achieving Vertical (Level 5) proficiency: through their research findings (e.g. 80% of leaders fail to move beyond Level 4), best practice cases, and an array of invaluable questions and challenges that each leader must address to achieve leadership maturity. This book is an invaluable map that can help any leader navigate the perils of leading complex organizations in a turbulent environment. Choosing to read this charming and illuminating book is a great strategic decision for any leader—the time spent will pay major dividends personally as well as professionally.

Roderick Gilkey, PhD
Professor in the Practice of Organization & Management, Goizueta Business School at Emory University
Professor of Psychiatry and Behavioral Sciences, Emory School of Medicine

"Satisfaction comes not from reaching the destination, but by continuing to grow." These wise and inspirational words by Keith and Karl remind us of the journey of our lives in which our *personality* is the *vehicle* and our *energy* is the *fuel*. Eigel and Kuhnert's meticulous blending of research, storytelling, and the use of personal examples makes "Finding Your Path to Effectiveness in Leadership, Life and Legacy" a valuable resource for anyone who want to chart their own course in effective leadership. Candidly, this book is a pioneering source that will enable you to build and follow your roadmap for achieving effective leadership.

Shweta Sharma Sehgal, PhD
Scholar at the Department of Business Economics, Delhi University

The MAP

YOUR PATH TO EFFECTIVENESS IN LEADERSHIP, LIFE, AND LEGACY

KEITH M. EIGEL, PhD
KARL W. KUHNERT, PhD

Cover design and interior formatting by Anne McLaughlin, Blue Lake Design

ISBN: 978-0-9907879-9-0
Published by Baxter Press, Friendswood, Texas
First printing 2016
Printed in the United States

Publisher's note: To ensure anonymity, names and details have been changed in many of the stories in this book.

DEDICATION

To your courageous journey of continuous growth.

To our families:

Leigh, Alexandra, Pete, John Thomas, and Ansley Eigel

Gay, Caroline, and Belle Kuhnert

To the journey and influence of Robert Kegan, a thinker and sharer
who has shaped both our journeys, and on whose shoulders
we stand. His influence is on every page of the book.

CONTENTS

PREFACE

by Keith Eigel

We are all leaders somewhere. Karl Kuhnert and I say this as people who have been trained in Industrial/Organizational Psychology—the psychology of business. You may not be an executive or manager in an organization, but you *are* a leader, either at home, with a group of friends, or informally with peers or coworkers in various situations. On a personal level you most likely make daily decisions to strengthen your most important relationships, grow in your knowledge and skills, and otherwise add value to life. For us, this influence with others (and even yourself) is our definition of leadership.

Our passion for the last twenty years has been to help leaders of every stripe realize their potential and maximize their effectiveness. My experience has been primarily with businesses, but the principles we will present in this book are just as effective and helpful for leadership in families, churches, nonprofits, and other settings. You don't have to be the CEO of a major corporation for your effectiveness as a leader to make a significant difference. Every person can apply these principles and take steps toward a more effective, meaningful, prosperous life.

The research we have done over the last couple of decades shows that the best single measure of leaders' effectiveness is where they currently are on their own developmental journeys[1]—that is, their present level of development. This statement is true across any industry, IQ, education, position, skill set, personality—you name it. Journeying well is what matters most, whether at home or work, in our social groups, in our community or country, or with friends, coworkers, employees, bosses, or peers.

Karl and I have focused our professional and personal lives on the application of this journey to every area of life. Before I even started graduate school, Karl had spent a full decade researching and making contributions to the field of understanding the developmental journey and leader effectiveness. I came back to academia late (around my thirtieth birthday). Karl was a young professor—only a few years my senior—and invited me to study under him as I pursued my doctorate. Something clicked. We became friends even as we became colleagues, albeit the kind of friends where one friend could give the other friend a failing grade—sort of a unique twist to friendship.

In 1996 we began to develop a curriculum to accelerate people's progress on their own developmental journeys. The concepts we present in this book are the foundation of the curriculum we use at The Leaders Lyceum, a training center to help executives and next-generation leaders accelerate their growth and realize more of their potential as leaders. *The Map* is an overview of the most critical components of effectiveness in leadership. The concepts are rooted in more than a half-century of research of how people continue growing into and through adulthood in ways that increase success, well-being, and satisfaction.[2]

Karl and I have led groups down this path for almost twenty years, and we have developed a rhythm that is experienced by others as an inviting but pointed conversation. In this book, we wanted to echo our interactive style of leading groups through these concepts, so I have written the content of the book from my own first-person perspective. Karl's contributions are points of wisdom, experience, and application interspersed throughout every chapter.

We hope that as you read through *The Map* you will be shaped by our insights, even as we have been shaped by the insights of our participants and each other. We also hope you will be moved to accelerate your growth and realize more of your potential in leadership, life, and legacy.

INTRODUCTION

by Karl Kuhnert

My journey in writing this book began a long time ago as a newly minted Ph.D. in his first academic position. I agreed to teach a class on organizational leadership. My problem was that contemporary academic literature to create such a course was, to put it politely, boring. To make class interesting, or at least hold the students' attention, I felt compelled to seek out the classics like Machiavelli, Lincoln, Martin Luther King, Jr., and Aristotle—all great leaders in their own place and time. While the titles of their books would fill the seats in my classroom, I was concerned about the course's lack of grounding in the current academic leadership research literature.

Sometime during that fall, a senior professor in my department asked me to join him in a game of tennis. I lacked any perceivable talent at tennis, yet I agreed to play to get to know him better. I remember being so hot and exhausted after the first set that I needed to buy time to catch my breath. I was stalling: between gulps of water and retying my shoelaces for the third time, I asked him what he was reading. He was a clinical psychologist, and from his book bag on the bench came a copy of Robert Kegan's *The Evolving Self*.[3] He explained the premise and how he had benefited from Kegan's insights.

I lost the match (and many more thereafter), but the book changed my life. I would like to say it was my openness to hearing what was new from my colleague that caused the transformation, although at first I listened only because I couldn't marshal enough energy to serve the next set. In my case, invention was the mother of necessity!

Through Kegan's book I found a new way to think about developing leaders and new ways to teach and research leadership.[4]

The book describes how we grow as adults, and more specifically, how we mature in our thinking over the course of life. We don't see the world as it is but as we are. I had been under the mistaken assumption that we stop growing in our capabilities after adolescence. Kegan helped me see that leadership has a trajectory (or, if you prefer a different metaphor, an evolution), and where you are in the process determines your effectiveness in leading others. Kegan's book was aspirational as well as inspirational. I learned many lessons, but perhaps the most significant is that leadership isn't about how much you know or what behaviors you engage in, but about who you are. The emphasis on "who you are" as a leader is important, but not surprising or new. What's new, what's actually revolutionary, is that "who you are" as a leader can develop along a clearly recognizable path of personal growth. But of course, to find and follow that path, we need a Map!

Throughout this book, you'll find my contributions in the gray boxes. The interactive nature of Keith's and my contributions reflects the same back and forth teamwork we employ when we develop leaders. It seems to be effective there, and I trust it will be equally effective in the pages of this book.

THE MAP OF YOUR LIFE

In our age of ever-improving GPS technology, maps are becoming more and more an anachronism. You can download numerous apps to get you from where you are to where you want to be, one simple step at a time. There is no need for context: for where you have been, how long it has taken to get there, and maybe not even where you're headed after you get to your next stop. And to be honest, that's how a lot of people live their lives. While trying to "get ahead" in a general sense, they keep attempting to advance from point to point with no discernable plan.

But if you want to get some context—see where you've been and how far you've come, and take a peek at the terrain that lies ahead—there's nothing like a paper map and a marker to trace your path and mark your course. You get a feel for your rate of progress, and you don't tend to spend so much time wandering aimlessly. If you choose, you can opt for a more scenic route occasionally, but by keeping before you how much distance is yet to be covered before your final destination, you won't unintentionally waste a lot of time along the way.

A GPS approach to life seems efficient, but it is actually limiting. Instead of hopping blindly from point to point, we hope you will consider the benefits of using a map for your life. We are all making the same basic journey, but as you will see in the following pages, there are any number of variables that will make your journey different from mine. By using the Map provided in this book, you will better understand and enjoy the events along the way. More importantly, you can finish your journey well without getting stalled or straying off course.

Chapter 1

PREPARING FOR THE JOURNEY

"The real voyage of discovery consists not of seeking new landscapes, but in having new eyes." —*Marcel Proust*

I was headed for the Promised Land. For a young man in Atlanta in 1984, that meant the California coast—a land of big waves, big wind, and big hair. It was also an entire continent away, a trip that would turn out to be a rite of passage.

The plan was for my buddy Mark and me to drive from Atlanta to Santa Barbara so we could surf and sail in the mighty Pacific with the big boys. We could drive to Nashville, hang a left, and follow I-40 all the way to California—pretty much a 2,300-mile straight shot. But to complicate things, my girlfriend (who would soon become my wife) was working at a retreat center in Gunnison, Colorado. It didn't seem that far out of the way to stop off and see her. We would be in the neighborhood, right? So our road trip turned into a 3,000-mile odyssey over the Mississippi, past the St. Louis arch, across the plains of Kansas, through the Rockies and the Grand Canyon, past the lights of Las Vegas, to our West Coast destination. I think the only thing we missed was Graceland.

A journey of such magnitude should not be undertaken without some semblance of planning. Those were the days before smartphones and widespread Internet, much less Garmin or MapQuest. We mapped out the journey to my California Promised Land on an old Rand McNally atlas. The map, I soon learned, provided much more than direction. It helped us plan for essentials—where we would need to stock up on gas and food, and when to start looking for affordable hotels. It also helped us maintain an appropriate pace, urging us farther down the road many times when we might rather explore any number of scenic stops along the way.

We would be driving my dad's Dodge Caravan—four cylinders, gold paint, brown side panels—and towing a ten-year-old, sixteen-foot Hobie Cat. The vehicle was ill-equipped to pull my half-restored sailboat up even a moderate incline, and we were headed for the Rocky Mountains. It wasn't quite the opening scene from the *Beverly Hillbillies*, but it was close. (I eventually towed that boat more than 6,000 miles and only sailed it twice, nearly sinking it both times.)

What's Your Destination?

Such is the lure of the Promised Land. When you get the call, you have to go. Bruce Springsteen wrote a song called "Promised Land" as a tribute to middle-class America. Dr. Martin Luther King, Jr. spoke of it in his famous "I Have a Dream" speech. In ancient times, the Promised Land was synonymous with the land of Canaan, a place of peace and prosperity God promised to Abraham and his descendants. In all cases, it's a place we look forward to reaching . . . eventually.

Although we each may have a different idea of what our Promised Lands might look like, we all want to get to that special place where we will be most free to create, to achieve, to live an abundant life. Whether at work or in our personal lives, it is the place where we can realize our highest level of effectiveness and satisfaction. Yet even as we pursue this ultimate destination, something inside of us suspects it will always—and probably *should* always—remain just beyond our grasp because a life well lived is really more about the journey than the destination.

How would you describe the gap between who you are and who you want to be? The journey of effective leaders is one of constantly identifying and closing that gap. The best leaders have a mindset for lifelong growth, making contributions in every sphere of life: at work, at home, with friends, and in their communities.

Some leaders lack a vision for personal development, unable to see a gap between who they are and who they want to be. In a sense they've already arrived at their destination, even though it's far short of where they could have gone with their talents. Not surprisingly, those people are seldom effective leaders over the long haul.

The journey of your life has a lot of parallels to my journey across the country. Our aim with this book is to help you anticipate and prepare for the detours and obstacles along the way and to help you travel farther and faster. Ultimately, satisfaction comes not from reaching the destination, but by continuing to grow—just ask those who feel they've "arrived" if they still feel that way a year later. Songwriter Dan Fogelberg put it beautifully:

> "The higher you climb, the more that you see.
> The more that you see, the less that you know.
> The less that you know, the more that you yearn.
> The more that you yearn, the higher you climb."[5]

This is the spiritual and developmental paradox: the people farthest along on the journey are the ones who have the clearest view of how much farther there is to go. Think about it. Which group is more likely to believe they have life all figured out—teenagers or grandparents? The point is we have the opportunity to keep growing, and the closer we are to what we might call our destination, the more perspective we have on how much possibility for growth lies ahead. Even so, as we progress, the perspectives of our experience give us an increasingly clear understanding that can contribute to the journeys of others. Those who have journeyed long and well in pursuit of their Promised Lands have many worthwhile experiences to describe. If we are willing to listen and learn, we can improve and perhaps streamline the journeys to our own Promised Lands. Similarly, what we learn on our own journeys can be helpful to others.

Journeying well is important because everyone is a leader in some sense. My father-in-law has been in ministry since his early twenties and, outside of having an assistant, has held no formal organizational leadership roles. Yet his effectiveness as a leader has mattered greatly to thousands of people whose lives have been affected by his counsel and encouragement over the years. My wife is a leader in many facets of our life, the most critical of which is her leadership with our four children. Her effectiveness in this arena matters not only to me and to her, but especially to our children and the people they eventually will lead. My twenty-three-year-old daughter is a leader among her group of friends, and her effectiveness in that role will have an impact on her life, their lives, and the lives of the people her friends will touch. The flip side, of course, is that *ineffectiveness* as leaders—in any walk of life—will have far-reaching consequences as well.

So the $64,000 question is what can we do to be more effective in the areas where our influence as leaders matters? Ultimately, the answer to the question is less about *what we do* than *where we are*—specifically, where we are on our journey through various developmental levels that characterize how we understand our worlds, ourselves, and others. In other words, our location—how much we have grown on our own journeys—has more to do with our effectiveness as leaders than the things we do.

Our *doing* flows out of our *sense of identity*. In other words, how we see ourselves and others determines our effectiveness as leaders. But this self-perception isn't static; it changes in predictable ways as we move through the stages of growth[6] . . . but only *if* we move through the stages of growth

Too often, leaders focus exclusively on performance and neglect the factors that shape identity, inner strength, and the character qualities of leadership. This is what we mean by the statement: "Who we are matters more than what we do."[7]

Certainly there are better and worse behaviors, better and worse values, even better and worse personality styles depending on the situation, but one hundred years of leadership research has left us wanting for a clear answer.[8] Resources like *The 21 Irrefutable Laws of Leadership*[9] are helpful in providing insight into the behaviors and abilities that characterize successful leaders, but frustrating because they don't really tell us how to get there. They don't answer the question about what matters most for us *to become* effective leaders.

Our passion is to help others become all they were created to be, and our desire is for this book to help you map out your life journey to go farther than you might ever expect. The concepts presented in this book have been supported by research and experience, and to the degree you can grab hold of them, you can accelerate your development and change the trajectory of your journey to fully become the individual and leader you are meant to be.

The Map can show us how to grow so that we see options we've never seen before. When we see more options, we often make better decisions. In one of our programs for next generation leaders, Sara felt conflicted. She wanted to attend a session we were doing on values, but ironically she also wanted to take her son his first day of kindergarten. She couldn't be in both places at the same time, and she saw only two choices. As she shared her dilemma, she realized there was a third option: Sara asked her husband if he could change his plans and take their son to school while she came to the session. Her husband was thrilled to help, her son was happy, and Sara felt both relief and joy. Actually, the morning became a landmark day for both parents. The dad enjoyed a day with their son he hadn't experienced with their other children, and Sara discovered she didn't have to take responsibility for every "mommy" decision. Suddenly, Sara had a more effective understanding of who she and her husband were as parents—true partners in creating a family. This is a far better outcome than merely following a "what we do" checklist strategy for parenting in a two-career household. Ultimately, it wasn't what she did differently that mattered; it was how she understood what she did differently that made her more effective.

A Long Trip Ahead

Just as a picture is worth a thousand words, metaphors are word pictures that say more than the words themselves can express. I have found the metaphor of "life as a journey" to be useful in communicating the complexity of adult human development and effectiveness.

While there are innumerable factors that make each of our life journeys unique, three key factors can dramatically affect your ability to reach your destination. Those factors are the *vehicle* you are driving (your personality), how much and what kind of *baggage* you have (your capabilities, or lack thereof), and how much *fuel* you have (your energy that drives developmental fitness). Even though these factors affect the journey, they aren't the journey themselves.

The Vehicle

Your personality is the vehicle for your trip. A jeep, a minivan, a sports car, a luxury sedan, and a pickup truck all have different features. What are your vehicle's strengths and weaknesses? My parents' minivan was only nine months old, so it was dependable and provided all the space we needed. Yet it had a weak engine and almost no ground clearance, so as we went through the Rockies I knew I needed to stick to well-paved highways and avoid back roads and steep hills whenever possible. Likewise, each personality has its strengths and weaknesses that remain stable and consistent over the course of our lives. As you plan your journey, you need to understand your potential and your limitations.

In making the journey, no single personality type has a noticeable advantage over another. In consulting with leaders at all levels of organizations, we find all personality types at every level of development. The type of vehicle may influence your route, but you will still make progress on the journey unless you're taking a road to growth that does not suit your strengths. Therefore, you need to work from your strengths to get the most out of what you have been given rather than try to be someone you are not. Know your strengths and struggles, and understand how they can facilitate or hamper your journey.

One client, a multinational company, had grown by buying smaller companies; however, the merged companies never reached their full potential in the larger company. In our leadership program, the executives of the merged companies realized for the first time they were all driving the same vehicle. That's right. All but one had identical personality profiles. Because they all saw the problems in front them from the same point of view, they were blind to many of the problems they needed to address to have a successful merger. As we explained the concept of the Map, the executives soon realized they needed all available vehicles—theirs as well as other, dissimilar vehicles—to achieve success. They discovered that the greatest wisdom comes from listening to people with very different points of view.

The Baggage

The baggage on your developmental journey includes the capabilities (knowledge, skills, and abilities) that enable you to seize opportunities and face challenges. Your intelligence, charisma, communication ability, management skills, likability, expertise, training, and the like all impact how effectively or ineffectively you are able to make progress on your journey.

"Baggage" may have a negative connotation for you. People say things like, "Their marriage broke up because he or she had too much baggage." Indeed, some of the baggage we carry may be detrimental to developmental progress. Yet in order to make progress on the journey, other baggage is not only helpful, but necessary. On my California trip, my flip-flops were well utilized, but the boat was deadweight and really held me back. The irony is I was more committed to the boat than the flip-flops.

The ability to effectively reduce or enhance the impact of strengths and weaknesses will vary from person to person, but your baggage is something that must be addressed in your personal development. The worst thing you can do is to ignore or turn a blind eye to the way your baggage may be affecting your ability to journey well. Even if you try to hide your baggage in the trunk, it will still weigh you down and limit how fast you can go and how far you can travel on a tank of fuel.

At every point we gain insight and skills, those things become part of the baggage we continue to take with us on our journey. For instance, a person who successfully addresses relational conflict can become a valued peacemaker on a corporate team, in a family, or among friends. And someone who has overcome financial collapse and found solid ground will have special empathy and sound advice for others who are drowning in debt.

> As you become more self-aware of your baggage, you'll be able to make adjustments to accelerate progress to your Promised Land. One of the best ways to create this self-awareness is by seeking feedback from others. Bosses, peers, employees, spouses, and children can be invaluable sources for evaluating your baggage. Some of their feedback will be encouraging, but some will be painful to hear. Be sure to listen to it all.[10]

The Fuel

When you buy a new car it comes with a tank of gas. Yet when you're taking a long road trip, you are not limited to the gas you have in your tank at the start. You can add fuel as you go along. When you are born, your *fuel* for life's journey is your level of developmental energy. Some people have more than others, and although you don't get to choose your initial level of energy, you can increase it.

For example, think of the most physically fit people you know. You've probably noticed their drive for physical fitness is fundamentally different from yours (unless, of course, you are the most physically fit person you know). In my case, that person is a buddy of mine named Van. If you asked Van if staying in great shape was something he makes himself do, he would say, "No, it's something I 'can't not' do." Unfortunately, I, like most people, have to be very intentional in my pursuit of increased physical fitness.

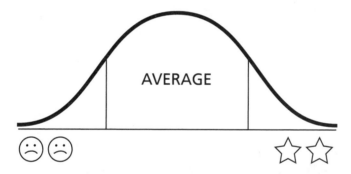

Do you remember the bell curve you hated to be graded on in high school? Well, our naturally physically fit friends likely fall in the very upper tail of that distribution. Those ten to fifteen percent of people seize their experiences and react to the world in such a way that they "can't not" develop.

The same distribution applies to developmental fitness. A small percentage of people lead the pack in a natural inclination toward developmental abilities, and at the other end of that bell curve are another ten to fifteen percent who have great difficulty developing. In fact, their development may even arrest, or stop. Those in between are average, and like it or not, will develop at what psychologists call a "normal rate" of development . . . unless some intentional intervention is made.

The good news is, just as we can adopt physical development techniques from those who are very physically fit, we can learn from those who have a high level of developmental fitness and accelerate the rate at which we grow. It's like putting fuel in your developmental tank, allowing you to accelerate your progress on your journey.

Intentionally accelerating personal, developmental growth has a lot of benefits. Not only will you become a better leader, whatever your role may be, but you will also live a more satisfied and energized life. That is what growth does, both physically and developmentally. It makes you stronger, more effective, and more satisfied. It is energizing because growth feeds on itself.

> Leadership is a muscle to be exercised and developed. The ongoing debate about whether leaders are born or made misses the point: if you don't stretch your leadership muscles, your influence atrophies and your effectiveness wanes. In sports, you can have all the natural physical ability in the world, but if you don't continue to train relentlessly, you won't be at the top of your athletic profession. The same principle applies in building strength, endurance, and flexibility as leaders in every sphere of life.

You're Going to Need a Map

The focus of the following chapters is all about journeying well and reaching your Promised Land. So much has already been written about personality, strengths and weaknesses, and best practice behaviors (your vehicle, baggage, and fuel respectively) that it would be redundant to cover that ground in this book. That does not mean that gaining a different set of skills or new self-awareness around these topics is not important. We should learn all we can and let the information increase our understanding of what we bring to the journey. However, even a comprehensive understanding of your vehicles, baggage, and fuel won't get you to your Promised Land without a roadmap.

This book unfolds the Map for your journey. It provides measurable landmarks to identify where you are now, and it provides strategies for accelerating progress that will allow you to maximize your effectiveness as a leader. It will enable you to make the best decisions for your own life first so you can then lead others well. Your vehicle, baggage, and fuel are what you need for the journey ahead.

When you know the Map—which shows where you are now and where you are going—you gain a context to help you understand your potential for growth. When you learn how to use the Map presented here, you gain an understanding of a theory that underpins your growth, meets you where you are, and can take you to your goal of greater effectiveness and satisfaction in leadership, life, and legacy.

Your growth—your quest to reach your Promised Land—has varied terrain and scenery that depends on the progress you have made, but being able to pinpoint your current location helps you navigate potential pitfalls so you won't miss the experience of something great. Knowing where you are starting from and where you want to go—in light of your vehicle, baggage, and fuel—will allow you to accelerate your progress on the journey.

Even though I can't become the strongest man in the world, I know that by applying the proper techniques and exercising discipline, I can realize more of my innate potential for physical strength. Similarly, the following chapters will provide tools and techniques that can put you on a track of accelerated development that will allow you to pursue your personal potential. These tools and techniques have helped thousands of others realize more of their potential in becoming the most developmentally fit leaders they can be. We don't get to choose many of the factors that affect us on our journeys. But here and now we can maximize our inherent potential based on our current locations, vehicles, baggage, and the fuel in our tank.

If you don't have any idea where you are going, you will get somewhere for sure, but odds are it won't be your Promised Land.

If each person reading this book were to choose his or her ultimate destination as a physical location, there wouldn't be as many Promised Lands as there are people, but there would be a lot of different ones for sure. We are complex beings, and, among many factors, our personalities, interests, skills and abilities, values, and backgrounds all influence the uniqueness of our destinations.

However, when we talk about the *developmental* journey, our Promised Lands have a great deal in common. All who continue to develop to the highest levels share a distinctly identifiable way of understanding themselves, their relationships, and their circumstances—a common way of seeing and understanding the world. They will differ in values, interests, abilities, personality, and the like, but not in the measurably different way they understand themselves, the world, and others.

> Virtually all of us know people who have gotten lost and are directionless. We also know people who have a purpose and know where they want to go in their life, and we realize this feat never happens by chance. No one reaches their destination alone. All of us need help along the way. Learning from wise people can help us make choices that lead to greater satisfaction, abundance, purpose, and productivity . . . to a destination with fewer regrets . . . in short, our Promised Land. The more specific you are about your destination, the greater the likelihood you will make decisions along the way that will take you where you really want to be.

Each of our routes and travel times to this destination—the highest level of understanding—will be different because our starting points vary. Where you are now may be quite different from where your best friend, spouse, colleague, or boss is. But by studying the Map, you can determine not only your current location, but also what your next steps need to be, and their order, to journey more effectively to your developmental Promised Land. Everyone will use the same Map, but for each person the route may be different. That's why it's critical to accurately identify your current location and to learn the options available in order to make the progress you want to make.

Fortunately, there are signposts along the way that can tell us where we are and help us identify our current level. Having the Map and learning the route can make the journey more predictable, more efficient, and even more fun. However, knowing the Map and the route is not the same as making the journey any more than studying the map for my cross-country journey with Mark was the same as making the trek.

Those who reach this Promised Land have something in common—they are all at the highest level of development. Over the following chapters, you will discover the characteristics of this destination in the context of the developmental Map. It would be nice if all you had to do was decide this destination was where you wanted to end up. It's an important first step, but there's a lot more to it. The vast majority of people never get there, but embarking on this journey with your eyes wide open greatly increases the odds that you will.

Is it worth it? Is the price we pay to make progress a reasonable investment? Everything worthwhile has a cost, and usually the greater the cost the greater the benefit. Journeying well may be the most difficult thing you ever do, but it can also be the most important and most rewarding. When you think of those who have made the biggest difference (whether on a global stage or in your organization or family), I bet you believe they lived their life well. Do you have the courage to pay the price they've paid?

Even when we look closely at those international leaders who have reached the highest measurable level of development, who got closest to the destination (think of Martin Luther King, Jr., Abraham

Lincoln, Gandhi, Mother Teresa),[11] we see that each of them was unique in training, skills, personality, and passion.

It's not a stretch to imagine how your own life experiences, upbringing, socioeconomic status, intelligence, education, and other factors contribute to the differences that make your journey unique. However, those differences don't make the Map itself any less accurate or helpful. Instead of taking my parents' minivan from Atlanta to California, I could have driven a sports car or pickup truck. The journey would have had a different feel in each case, but the roadmap would have been a constant. In other words, we can embrace the usefulness of the Map and still account for the impact our differences have on making each of our journeys unique.

Thoreau said it best: "If you don't know where you are going, any road will get you there." How many of us are looking for a road to a more productive life? How many even know that road exists? How many of us are too overwhelmed with daily demands of life to think about taking a road, any road, much less a road less traveled?

I can't count the number of times I've said to myself and anyone within earshot, "I can't take on one more thing!" The purpose of this book isn't to give you more items for your "to do list." There are no "irrefutable laws" to follow or reminders of things to do or say scrolling across your computer screen.

We wrote this book to help you make better sense of the motivations of people around you and help you to understand the demands of your role in a complex world. The book is based on twenty-five years of our research and more than fifty years of the research of others. Our hope is that you see yourself in the principles and the stories we tell. Leadership is complex, challenging, and invigorating. All of us have much to learn. Quite possibly, certain concepts in this book will propel you to the next level of effectiveness. We're offering more than a list of behaviors to perform; we're offering a new way of seeing.

People depend on you to lead with a blend of wisdom, strength, and understanding. We're offering a Map, and we're suggesting a path, but you have to take the steps. Your path forward (like everyone's) is both threatening and thrilling. The stakes are high, but the rewards are sweet.

Consider This . . .

1. When you think of "Promised Land," what comes to mind for you? Hint: How are you contributing to others and to life? (You may have more than one response as you consider work, family, faith, etc.) What are you currently doing to progress toward your Promised Land(s)?

2. In what area(s) of life do you see yourself as a leader? How would you evaluate your current level of effectiveness in each case?

3. Step back and examine yourself. How would you describe your vehicle (personality), baggage (knowledge, skills, and abilities), and fuel (level of developmental energy)?

4. After you write an assessment of the necessary elements for your journey (in #3), discuss your conclusions and questions with three trusted friends or family members to see if they agree with your assessment. In their responses, what surprised you and what confirmed your findings? What did they think you were hiding?

5. As you see yourself more clearly, what do you think will be your biggest challenges as you undergo your life's journey?

Chapter 2

THE VIEW FROM 30,000 FEET

When Mark and I set off on our cross-country expedition to California, we counted on the double-page spread at the front of my old Rand McNally atlas that showed the whole country, providing a great overview of what it would take to progress to our ultimate destination. Yet we soon learned to appreciate the individual state maps with the detailed insets of the major cities that included specifics we needed to know along the way. The more we dug in and studied the individual sections, the clearer the obstacles and challenges of any particular portion of the journey became.

When we needed to reorient ourselves after navigating through a busy city, we went back to the overview to get a sense of how the smaller pieces fit into the big picture. We still experienced surprises, detours, and other unexpected discoveries along the way, but the maps created enough reference to help navigate even the most significant ones pretty darn effectively.

Likewise, as we begin to understand our developmental Map, it is helpful to start with a high-level overview of the journey—the

30,000-foot view. If I had backed out of my driveway in Atlanta and immediately started looking for signs directing me to Santa Barbara, I would never have gotten there. I had to consult the map and determine that my journey must first take me from Atlanta to St. Louis, then on to Salina (Kansas), to Gunnison (Colorado), to Las Vegas, and *then* to Santa Barbara. Only when I got close to each of those cities did I begin to gather specific information to add to the map overview.

Onward and Upward: Lateral and Vertical Growth

On your journey through life, the question is: Will you just react to things that happen to you along the way and let the whims of circumstance take you where they will, or will you intentionally chart your course? If your answer is the latter, a map will be a necessary asset.

The Map we offer you is drawn from over fifty years of research in developmental psychology. I realized I had hit on something of critical importance to leadership almost twenty years ago. I saw that the people I admired most—from world-changing leaders, to my grandfather and favorite college professor, to the most effective leaders of organizations—all had one thing in common. They had all reached the highest level of personal development.

The idea that there are distinct levels of development (think of them as *mileposts*) is not new. But as I sought to apply this theory of development to leadership, I read everything I could get my hands on about leader effectiveness. What was it that separated great leaders from their lower-performing peers? Was it knowledge? Personality? A special set of skills? (In other words, was it their vehicle, or baggage, or fuel?) The answer in each case was no.

Their vehicles, baggage, and fuel didn't predict or explain their effectiveness any more than the type of car I drive predicts my ability to get to the store. The more I read, the more I kept coming back to the same thing: the people I admired most had achieved meaningful influence because they were at a different level developmentally. Their effectiveness was not determined by knowledge, personality, or skills. In fact, those three factors varied greatly. Additionally, many other leaders with similar knowledge, skills, and personalities who led in similar circumstances and roles were not nearly as effective. Some were downright ineffective. The thing that distinguished the great leaders was that they understood themselves, others, and their world at a measurably higher level on this developmental trajectory. They were farther along on the Map—closer to their Promised Lands.

Developmental psychologists have studied for decades how we grow in our understanding of our environments and relationships over time.[12] This growth is measurable and predictable, and the findings apply to all of us. Just as I began my journey to the West Coast by focusing on the big-picture overview of the roadmap, we will begin with a big-picture overview of the developmental Map. That way, as we identify landmarks along the developmental road, we will more easily see the context in which they sit and why they are important, both for ourselves and for those in our circles of influence. We can think of each of these landmarks along the way as a new level of development, and the better we understand the characteristics of each level, the less we will have to guess where we are currently or what our best next steps should be.

In the realm of developmental psychology, many experts identify five major levels of development.[13] On the developmental Map these are like big metropolitan areas on a roadmap. The five major levels are as different as the cities of St. Louis, Salina, Gunnison, Las Vegas, and Santa Barbara were on my cross-country trek. In the context of development, these levels are progressively distinct ways of understanding our circumstances, ourselves, and our relationships—or as I will often refer to them, our worlds, ourselves, and others.

Only by identifying your specific location on the developmental Map can you determine your exact starting point and then clarify the next steps to enable you to accelerate progress on the journey to your final destination. These levels correlate approximately with age, but only as an average of the population at any given level. Your age does not automatically determine your level, although you can consider it a starting point to understanding the general level at which you might be if you have been developing at a "normal" pace. It's like entering only a state, without a city designation, into your GPS—it may get you in the ballpark, but it won't be very helpful at getting you to a specific destination.

Progress can be a deceptive word. There are two distinct ways to understand how we continue growing in adulthood: *Laterally* and *Vertically*.[14] Let's consider making progress in the area of conflict resolution. Lateral development adds to what you know and do. For example, you can gain new knowledge or learn a new skill set in an afternoon. You read a book or take a class that teaches five steps for conflict resolution, and Lateral development occurs the moment you learn the steps. Most traditional learning environments—schools, corporate training sessions, seminars, and books—foster Lateral development.

Vertical development involves more than learning. It is transformational change in your understanding or perspective of what you know, what you do, or who you are.[15] Rather than learning five steps for conflict resolution, for instance, Vertical development would entail understanding the purpose or value of conflict in a new, different, and increasingly more complete way.

Vertical development changes how you think about conflict, and it also fundamentally changes you. When you grow and change Vertically, your understanding of the people in the conflict also grows and changes.[16] You see the dispute as a challenge rather than a calamity, and you realize each person can learn valuable lessons from facing the reality of the conflict rather than demanding to win, ignoring it, or running away. As we mature in our understanding of conflict, we are more capable of finding "win/win" solutions. Growth affects our abilities in all levels of conflict, from personal to international. The significant conflicts we face in the world, such as the Middle East turmoil or global warming, can only be solved with a more mature way of thinking.

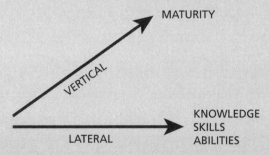

The "big idea" in this chapter is the distinction between growing Laterally and growing Vertically. This contrast has been studied in the leadership research literature for the past several years. Lateral development is "acquired knowledge" and Vertical development is "insight that changed you." Most of what goes on in academic classrooms, or from watching shows like *Animal Planet,* is acquired knowledge. Students and viewers are passive learners who absorb facts about accounting practices or the mating habits of hippos, respectively. What we learn Laterally is still important. Acquired knowledge to pass a CPA exam, for example, is a high barrier to enter the accounting profession. Passing the exam opens doors to new possibilities. But Vertical development, the "insight that changed you," is much more valuable— especially when trying to get promoted to partner in the accounting firm.

This distinction between Lateral and Vertical growth is critical when developing leaders. An effective leadership development program is one that changes you Vertically, not just Laterally. It's not enough to provide "best practices" around what exceptional leaders do unless that content is delivered and integrated in a way that fundamentally changes the way the participants sees themselves in the context of leading others. The experience has to actually transform the participant—which is Vertical development. Creating opportunities for Vertical challenges in a leadership development program requires gifted facilitators who can generate a great deal of awareness. This is the process the most effective teachers use every day in the classroom, and what experienced mentors and managers use with the people around them. Vertical transformation doesn't take place over the course of a day or a week, but often over months and sometimes years.

I've had the good fortune to present leadership concepts to my college's alumni groups. I like to mingle after the presentations, and my favorite question to ask alumni is, "Why do you give money and donate your time to the college?" The most frequent answer—if they let me dig deeply enough—is that their experiences in college propelled their growth. They tell me about meaningful relationships they created and personal obstacles they overcame. They remember long nights studying and degrees they earned, but those factors aren't transformative. They are deeply moved to donate their time and money to universities because they acquired the most important lessons in life during their time in college. Alumni who give back to their universities recognize that they became better versions of themselves during their college years. In all my conversations with alumni, I've never heard any of them wax eloquently and passionately about the deep meaning they derived from a chemistry or sociology class, but they often recount stories of an instructor or a friend who touched and ultimately changed their lives. The experience of Vertical development is why people "pay it forward."

Not all students or potential leaders experience a transformative Vertical experience. We are, after all, at different places on the developmental Map and are likely to interpret similar experiences quite differently. As one of my mentors said, "It's not the experience that is important, but what you make of that experience that matters."

Knowledge isn't enough. In our leadership training (and in all venues where leaders have an impact on others), we provide content in a context that's both challenging and supportive. Leaders help others put on new lenses to see situations and people in a very different way. Then, threats become opportunities. But first the *leader* needs to put on new lenses. As Gandhi famously stated, "You must be the change you wish to see in the world."

This effort to grow Vertically can seem very abstract at first blush because we have spent most of our lives attempting to (and being evaluated on the ability to) increase our knowledge, skills, and abilities—more Lateral development. So let us start with a quick Lateral view of Vertical development:

Vertical growth is measurable. You can know where you are on your Vertical journey.

Vertical growth takes place in a predictable order. All of us grow in the same expected stages. You do not skip levels of Vertical growth, nor do you go backward.

Vertical growth is related to chronological age, but is not determined by it. Actually, the older you get, the more likely you are to stop or arrest growth.

The higher the level of Vertical development, the more effective you are in all aspects of life and leadership. In fact, no single factor better predicts your effectiveness than where you are on your Vertical journey.

Perhaps the best everyday term for Vertical development is *maturity*. When we grow in maturity we understand ourselves, others, and circumstances in increasingly more comprehensive and effective ways. We are able to achieve a more complete perspective the more mature we are. This maturity is the process of Vertical development, and it will be the focus of the rest of this book.

Lateral development can be thought of as *what we know*. Vertical development is not *what* we know, but *how we know* what we know. Vertical growth doesn't necessarily change what we know, but it does change how we interpret or understand that knowledge. Typically, if we keep growing, our perspective on the world around us continues to change as we go through our formative years, move through our teens into our twenties, cross midlife, and ultimately enter our senior years. We call this progression Vertical development.

Consider a seventy-year-old lifelong political activist (Democrat or Republican, take your pick). At twenty he was probably considerably more idealistic, accepting the party platform at face value and passionately convinced that his party's ideals were the key to solving the nation's problems. Fifty years later his core beliefs may not have changed much at all, yet life experiences have challenged his *way* of understanding those ideals. He has struggled with seeing political initiatives lead to undesired outcomes, the limitations of what any political party can actually accomplish, and numerous other challenges. Yet those very challenges paradoxically turned an idealistic twenty-year-old into a stronger and less easily shaken mature adult. His Lateral development (the content of his ideology, values, and platform) has changed little over the years. But his Vertical development (his perspective) has changed dramatically.

Vertical development is changing who we are in relationship to the problem.

Challenge: The Key to Vertical Development

Vertical development doesn't happen when everything is going your way. Why would you change when things are great? Vertical development usually occurs in the wake of challenging experiences. If you look back over your life and identify those experiences that challenged you most, you probably recognize that they helped you develop a more mature and effective understanding of yourself, others, and the world. They helped you grow Vertically.

Challenging experiences are different from problems. Problems are something to be solved. We can learn something new (Lateral development) to fix a problem, but a challenging situation goes deeper and requires a Vertical response.

When we use the word *challenge* instead of *problem*, we change our perception of reality and how we shape our response. Quite often, problems can be solved with a single discrete solution. A common impulse is to try to solve our deeper, broader, more significant challenges in the same way we solve our problems: with a quick answer, or by ignoring them and hoping they'll go away. But we need to lean into our challenges over time, with more thought and tenacity. Problems may need only a Lateral solution, but challenges require a Vertical response.

As an example, let's return to the issue of conflict with a colleague. In your twenties, such conflict is both a problem and a challenge. The problem is the conflict itself—you want a solution. The challenge is that the conflict keeps you up at night and unsettles your days. A Lateral development solution—learning and applying steps of conflict resolution—can solve the immediate problem, but the challenge will continue to exist. Future conflicts will continue to unsettle you. It is this type of challenge that actually helps you grow Vertically as you learn to deal with yourself in the problem more than just the problem at hand.

One leader I interviewed expressed this truth perfectly when he said, "Look, at my company we all like to get along with one another, but we can still have conflict at work and go out that evening and play tennis together. Conflict is still present, but there is no tossing and turning all night, no wondering, 'Are we okay?'"

What creates such growth? The same thing that develops all of us Vertically—learning to make sense of a challenge in a new way. These types of challenges don't really get solved; rather, they wind up *solving us* in a sense. Vertically, we outgrow them by making sense of them in a better, more complete way until the situation that formerly challenged us is no longer challenging. As adults we can look back and see that what challenged us in our teenage years is no longer challenging—not because as teens we learned some simple, how-to steps to solve the challenge, but because the challenge created Vertical growth.

Challenging life experiences either accelerate or arrest Vertical growth. The more challenging the experience, the greater its potential to bring about Vertical development. When I crossed the Rocky

Mountains I was in a modern vehicle on a good road, but it wasn't hard to understand why the pioneers in their Conestoga wagons traveled primarily on the plains. The mountains appeared too ominous. Similarly, any number of threatening circumstances can stall us at various points in our life journeys. But if we muster the determination to get over those mountains to the other side . . . my, what a different perspective we will have!

This concept is not new. In the middle of the first century a.d., Paul from Tarsus wrote in a letter that, "suffering [or challenge] produces endurance, and endurance produces character, and character produces hope" (Rom. 5:3-4). Hope, in the context of Vertical development, is the expectation that a better, more complete, more mature understanding lies ahead. At about the same time, James, the brother of Jesus of Nazareth, put it this way: "Consider it a sheer gift, friends, when tests and challenges come at you from all sides. . . . Don't try to get out of anything prematurely. Let it do its work so you become mature and well-developed, not deficient in any way" (James 1:2-4, MSG).

Ralph Waldo Emerson shrewdly observed, "Bad times have a scientific value. These are occasions a good learner would not miss."

Sixty years of modern psychological research has shown these insights on the value of challenges to be true. When we persevere through adversity (challenge), we develop character (maturity) and continue to grow.

On October 31, 2003, thirteen-year-old Bethany Hamilton went surfing with her best friend and the best friend's father and brother. At about 7:30 a.m., with sea turtles all around and her arm dangling in the water, a fifteen-foot tiger shark attacked, severing her left arm at the shoulder. Her friend's family got her to shore, fixed a tourniquet on the stump of her arm, and rushed her to the hospital. She had lost sixty percent of her blood, but was stabilized and released from the hospital a week later.

Bethany's story has been documented in the media and through her book, *Soul Surfer*.[17] I don't think it is a stretch to say that most teenagers would have responded to the loss of an arm with "Why me?" or "This isn't fair!" But Bethany was quoted as saying, "Surfing isn't the most important thing in life. Love is. I've had the chance to embrace more people with one arm than I ever could with two."[18]

This young girl endured an intense challenge and persevered through it, resulting in accelerated growth. She was somehow able to incorporate some of the most complex and painful realities of life and come through them with a level of understanding you would only expect to see from someone three or four times her age.

Nobody signs up for that kind of growth: "Yes, I'll take one death in the family and some serious illness, please." Of course not! Yet because we have no control over when challenging times come our way, our growth trajectory is sometimes accelerated by the unpredictable capriciousness of circumstance. Other times we may *choose* to hasten our maturity as we learn to willingly embrace difficult challenges and growth opportunities. Subsequent chapters will have more to say about this.

If you review the challenges you have faced in your past, you will probably see that the ones you confronted were resolved in less time than those you avoided or put off. Persevering by leaning into challenges (rather than avoiding them) is necessary for Vertical development to occur. We often have no other option than to persevere when a challenge is unavoidable (getting fired, battling illness, losing a loved one, etc.), but we can also persevere intentionally when a challenge is avoidable. When we do, we accelerate Vertical growth with intention.

Still, it takes time to process challenges that contradict your current understanding in a way that will result in Vertical growth. Vertical development does not take place overnight. Suppose you work out for thirty minutes, twice a week, for six months. You will invest twenty-five hours into exercise, and you will be measurably stronger and more physically fit as a result. However, if you skip working out for six months and try to get in your twenty-five hours over a single weekend, you will certainly be sore and probably injured. What's worse is you won't be in any better shape on Monday.

The same principle applies to developmental fitness. Small steps that lean into an otherwise avoidable challenge build strength of understanding *over time*. In this way developmental fitness is accelerated beyond the whims of circumstance and results in a more comprehensive, mature, and effective understanding—one that can make sense of things that previously challenged you.

Let me offer a personal example. When I was growing up, I was an average athlete—good at a lot of sports, but not great at any. I wanted to improve, so many times I tried on my own to find that outstanding "inner athlete" I was convinced resided somewhere inside me.

When I felt particularly ambitious and dedicated, I added a new set of weights, bought a treadmill, or worst of all, signed a contract for a gym membership that I seldom used after the first couple weeks.

I badly damaged my right knee in college and by the time I was thirty-eight, I had to have most of it replaced with metal and plastic. The surgeon said my recovery time would be significantly reduced if I worked out with a strength trainer, so three months prior to the surgery, I began meeting with a trainer twice a week. He showed me how to build strength without aggravating my knee injury. But in addition, I benefited from built-in accountability because I bought blocks of the trainer's time and scheduled twice-a-week appointments. Soon I realized this approach to fitness training was different from any of my previous efforts.

The doctor was right. I recovered from surgery in record time. I was able to flex my muscles and actually get up and walk the day of the surgery. The average recovery time was eight to twelve weeks, but I was gingerly hitting golf balls after three.

Becoming stronger had been a goal of mine since high school, but nothing I tried before hiring a trainer produced the desired results. Sadly, it didn't last. After I completed my physical therapy, I immediately began to slip back into my undisciplined ways. When it came time for my workout, I always seemed to find something more urgent I needed to do. It didn't take me long to see that continuing to have a trainer would make a big difference for me. I tend to be spontaneous, and I like to be involved in a lot of things. But when I was paying $45 per session, in advance, to someone who had a twenty-four-hour cancellation policy, I found I was too well-intentioned to cancel that far in advance and too cheap to not show up.

I had to admit, reluctantly, that I would never be better than an average athlete without help. It wasn't a sign of tragic failure, just my nature. But, since discovering what worked for me, I've been able to respond to physical challenges more effectively. I can do things now that I couldn't do in the past. This development requires a significant investment of both time and money (about $4,500 a year and four hours a week), but intentionally submitting myself to the accountability and systems of the trainer helped me become stronger and more physically fit than I've ever been—and without getting injured or bored.

I've transferred this lesson to other areas of my life. Because I've accepted the fact that I'm part of the majority of people who are average in the ability to grow Vertically, I can begin to put systems in place, commit the necessary investment of time and money, and get the help I need to grow to the highest levels of development at a pace that maximizes my potential.

Vertical Development: Lenses and Levels

There are five major levels of Vertical development. For the sake of simplicity, I will refer to them simply as Level 1, Level 2, etc. We move from one level to the next as we learn to see the world around us from a more advanced perspective. Think of your current level of understanding as a lens through which you observe what's going on around you. When events or new information challenge your understanding in such a way that the lens no longer gives you a clear and focused image of the experience in a way that you can fully understand it, you have two choices: (1) You can ignore the contradiction and continue to view the experience through your (now blurry) current lens; or, (2) You can develop a new lens that allows you to make sense of the situation more clearly. The latter choice is Vertical development.

Your lens, like a contact lens attached to the eye, is the filter and focusing mechanism for everything you see. You are never able to take a perspective on your current lens, which changes as you grow in a predictable and orderly way, each time helping you focus more clearly and completely. Each successive lens, or level of Vertical growth, makes better sense of your world than your previous ones did, because each time you grow to a new level you still have access to your previous lenses. This additive effect is why our understanding becomes more complete, true, and effective as we continue to grow.

So at this point let's take an initial look at the five stages of Vertical growth and the lens used for each one. Each level is like a different city on the way to your Promised Land. At each one, you will discover new things about yourself and experience significant growth, yet if you don't continue your forward progress, you can get stuck at almost any of these points. In later chapters we will decrease our altitude and be much more specific about each of these levels.

When I'm at lunch with an executive, I draw a diagram of the levels of development on a napkin. When I speak at leadership seminars and conferences, I often use a whiteboard to draw a diagram of the levels. It looks something like this:

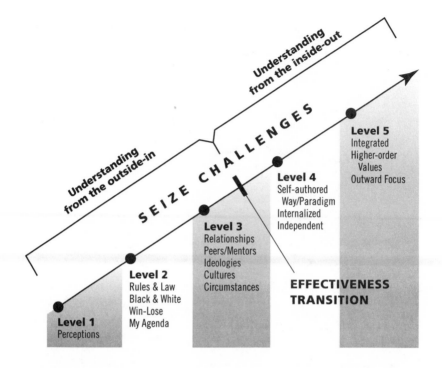

Level 1: Perception Is Reality

Technically, we are born into an initial level of development, Level 0 (zero). Jean Piaget, the renowned child psychologist, was one of the first to explore this stage. He verified what most parents know by instinct: infants understand their world limited by what they can sense or immediately experience. It's why peekaboo works with babies. You hide your face and you effectively go away. You uncover it and Oh-my-gosh! The stimulus actually defines the infants' understanding of themselves, others, and the world.

However, the first major transition of life is witnessed by any parent who experiences the repeated "no's" of a child going through the "terrible twos"—the child is moving to Level 1, which is where we will start. This transition from infants to toddlers can be a difficult one. Challenge and contradiction result when the child no longer wants to be identified by the immediate stimulus (including Mom or Dad) telling him what to do. Thus, the "No!"

Through the Level 1 lens, perception is reality. My wife and I were blessed with a bonus baby in our early forties—she's the family mascot. As a young child, Ansley was a joy and constant source of entertainment. During her fourth year, she perfectly exemplified that her perceptions were her reality. You couldn't convince her that her dolls in the backseat on the way to preschool weren't real. She insisted that I was twenty years old. (She missed it by more than half.) But there was no point arguing with her about what she perceived to be true because to her it *was* true. Because a preschool, Level 1 understanding is limited to children's perceptions of what is true, they will happily give you a dime for three pennies, but you can't win an argument with them. That said, after a while, peekaboo isn't much fun with preschoolers. The lens through which they see the world is no longer limited to the experience of the immediate stimulus. Now they can reflect back on that previous lens and use it to make more effective sense of the world than an infant, and the additive nature of a previous lens and a current lens begins the effectiveness journey.

Level 2: The Black and White World

At Level 2 we begin to realize that there is reality independent of our perceptions. During our formative years (roughly ages seven through twelve) we learn what is becoming our Level 2 understanding from outside sources: parents, family, elementary school teachers, and the like. In lieu of good outside sources, children will turn to whatever source is given the authority to speak into their understanding of self, others, and world, including the Nickelodeon and Disney channels.

By the time Level 2 children enter middle school, they have a very concrete, either/or understanding of choices, values, and people. Learning is reinforced by rewards and consequences, so it becomes very win/lose, with a powerful desire to either achieve the win or avoid the loss. This simplistic, me-first, my-agenda way of seeing things is tolerable when Level 2 understanding is age-appropriate. Note that I didn't say it was *easy*, I said it was *tolerable*, which is why I personally think middle school teachers and administrators are some of the most underappreciated people in society. However, this Level 2 mentality is far less tolerable when exhibited by those whose Vertical growth stops but their aging doesn't, as we will see in later chapters.

When I was learning the theories of child development in graduate school, my oldest child, Alex, was seven years old (Level 2) and our second child, Pete, was four (Level 1). They were both sitting at our kitchen counter, and I had three cookies for them to share. Because Alex was older and bigger than Pete, I gave her two cookies and gave Pete one. As you can imagine, this cookie distribution strategy didn't go over well with Pete. When crocodile tears started rolling down his chubby cheeks I quickly applied my newly acquired knowledge of child development. I broke Pete's cookie in two pieces and asked him if that was better. His tears dried, he smiled, and he gave Alex a smug look that said, "That's what I'm talking about." Alex, on the other hand, gave me a look that let me know that she was sure she had the world's dumbest brother. Through Pete's lens, which relied solely on his perceptions, two half-cookies were the same as two cookies. But through Alex's Level 2 lens, cookies had actual mass, and simply breaking one in half didn't make two.

Alex's understanding had nothing to do with any information she might have acquired in a second grade science class about mass and volume (which would be Lateral development). Instead, she had developed to a level where she could look back and see that what she *perceived* to be true at any given moment was not necessarily what *was* true. These are facts that can be counted on to make sense of the world. Her Level 2 understanding was an improvement over her previous level of understanding because she had both her perceptions (Level 1) and her facts (Level 2) to help her understand and make sense of the situation, whereas Pete's lens was limited to his perceptions.

Level 2 adults who lead teams are anything but cute. A middle school leadership style in a forty-year-old body creates organizational havoc and distress among those who report directly to a Level 2 leader. To them, you're a competitor—a potential threat to their promotion, their success, their bonus. They still need to prove how good they are, and specifically, how much better they are than you. Actually, arrested development at Level 2 can be very scary; it can border on sociopathic. Another book I would like to write would have the title *Sociopaths I Have Known In Business*. These would be the Level 2s I've known in positions of authority.

Level 3: From Outside-In to Inside-Out Thinking

Eventually the simple, rules-oriented, reward-and-consequence motivated way of seeing things will be challenged by experience. Level 2 teens will be challenged when they realize that getting their way is actually not the real win—the bigger win is when they suspend their own agenda to coordinate it with others. They begin to empathize and see the world through the eyes of others. This new, emerging, Level 3 understanding begins for most during their teenage years.

As we grow from Level 2 to Level 3, a number of new influences begin to hold sway. Because parents and teachers played such a key role in the creation of the Level 2 understanding, their input is often discounted in the initial transition toward Level 3. Instead, peers will gain inordinate influence—thus the peer pressure of the teenage years. As our teenage years draw to a close, the influence of teachers, coaches, and peers will yield to some degree to the social structures and organizations with which we are affiliated. Political and religious ideologies, culture, media, and the norms of the organizations we associate with will strongly shape our understanding of the world.

As young adults, most will have come into the fullness of Level 3 understanding, but that wholesale adoption of the outside sources will eventually be challenged by experiences, other perspectives, new information, and other influences that contradict our Level 3 understanding. A major shift in thinking occurs. Until this point growth and development has had an Outside-In emphasis. We may have a wide assortment of influences, but the common bond is that we take to heart what valued others tell us.

Most of us who approach our mid-thirties will begin to see the limitations of the Level 3 understanding our outside sources have provided. We begin to realize, "The world isn't as simple and answers aren't as clear as I thought," and we begin to ask ourselves, "What do I really hold to be true?" The attempt to answer that question for ourselves will begin the journey into Level 4 understanding, a new way of understanding the world from the *inside out* instead of *outside in*.

This increasingly Inside-Out way of seeing the world can be thought of as our developing paradigm—not a paradigm shaped by the influences of outside sources like corporate culture, society, and political or religious ideologies, but by our own "self-authored" way of seeing self, others, and the world. (By *self-authored*, I mean that you take ownership and responsibility for the kind of person you want to become, even as you realize you will still need others to help you realize that aspiration.)

Quite often, Level 3 managers avoid making decisions at all costs. Their default decision-making preference is to take a vote—not because they live in a democracy (a convenient excuse), but rather so they won't be responsible for the outcome. If the decision based on the vote doesn't succeed, the Level 3 leader can claim, "We all decided . . . so you can't blame me." Indecision and waffling are hallmarks of the Level 3 leader.

Level 3 leaders also have trouble with honest relationships. Have you ever had conflict with a colleague who sought you out the next day and asked sheepishly, "Are we okay?" If that colleague is Level 3, he wasn't so much concerned about you as he was concerned about your perception of him. Meaningful human connections require give and take, mutual compassion, and understanding, but Level 3 leaders are too defined by their relationships, and in this codependency don't experience those benefits.

Level 4: The Effectiveness Transition

By Level 4 the Inside-Out perspective on life has fully developed. We call this change from Outside-In to Inside-Out the "effectiveness transition." When we make this shift, we become measurably more effective in leading across all areas of our lives. In fact, research on Vertical development and leader effectiveness shows it is not until we are more Level 4 than we are Level 3 that we are seen as being effective in our leadership roles, formal or informal.

As we become Level 4, we are no longer satisfied with the adopted, Level 3 understanding of our various outside influences. Our Inside-Out, Level 4 understanding is much more complete, accurate, and effective because we can take an objective look at the benefits and limitations of the previous three levels (and even the benefits and limitations of peekaboo). At Level 4 we are able to realize the influence of each of our previous lenses and see how we have arrived at our current, self-authored understanding. In addition, we can acknowledge the shortcomings of those previous lenses, which allows us an even more comprehensive and accurate Inside-Out understanding of the world.

Prior to Level 4, leadership ability is usually based on intelligence, expertise, communication skills, charisma, etc.—all of which are Lateral knowledge, skills, and abilities commonly found in bright college students who are usually Level 3 at best. However, what Level 4 leaders may lack in charisma, communication skills, intelligence, or expertise, they make up for in maturity and self-awareness, which makes them more effective leaders. Think of the smartest twenty-four-year-olds you know. Do you want any of them leading your organization? They may have all the Lateral development required, but not the maturity that comes only with Vertical development.

You may remember the line by Forrest Gump: "Now Bubba had told me everything about shrimpin', but you know what I found out? Shrimpin' is tough."

When I first started teaching the levels of leadership, I found it much easier to lecture about the levels than to actually try to live Levels 4 and 5, because at the time, I wasn't equipped for them. Learning to lead from the inside out isn't easy. To paraphrase Forrest, "Livin' at Level 4 is tough."

Living an "Inside-Out" life is challenging because I'm ultimately responsible for my decisions. If I'm unhappy with my life, my life's work, or my social status in the community, I don't blame my university, wife, boss, barber, or anyone else. I don't blame others (or events) for my failures, passivity, or unhappiness.

Think about the person in your life, at work or at home, who is most difficult for you to lead—or even to be with in the same room for more than fifteen minutes. Who is responsible for your discomfort . . . and maybe your resentment? Very few leaders I coach think they're responsible for such strained and broken relationships, so they make no effort to repair them.

At Level 4, we take responsibility for those relationships; we don't blame others and we don't ignore the problems. If those relationships are to improve, it's our responsibility to make them better. But first, we have to change ourselves.

Taking responsibility for one's own decisions isn't the norm in American business, but it's the way effective leaders lead. Our Outside-In culture encourages assigning blame for our problems to parents, drugs, videogames, schools, or anything else.

One of my favorite quotes is from John Wooden, the legendary basketball coach, who said, "The worst you can do for the ones you love the most is what they could and should do for themselves." Wooden, like so many Inside-Out leaders, knew that growing responsibility in others is the key to building successful teams and organizations. Teams win when teammates know and accept their responsibilities, and teams lose when they point the finger and blame each other. (Once when I shared Wooden's statement in a group, a woman in the audience asked me if *not* completing her son's homework each night was a good application she could make. Before I could reply, "Yes, it is!" a collective gasp from the group answered for me.)

Living an Inside-Out life is challenging, but it's also very freeing: I can pursue any good and meaningful goal. What I accomplish is only limited by me. This feeling isn't like picking an item off a restaurant menu; it's writing the menu yourself.

One of the biggest challenges at Level 4 is to keep growing Vertically. The shift from Outside-In to Inside-Out thinking, and the effectiveness that results, make it all too easy to double down on our self-authored paradigm by force-fitting challenges and contradictions through the Level 4 lens rather than allowing those challenges and contradictions to provide fuel to take us to a Level 5 understanding.

Maturing in your leadership is one of the most challenging aspects of life. It doesn't happen without challenge and contradiction—and giving up some long-cherished certainties. Level 4 leaders have arrived at this point of development by carefully crafting their values and learning from their vast wealth of experiences, yet past successes can become a barrier to future growth. Most Level 4 leaders get stuck at this point. They're victims of their own success, and they aren't open to new ways of seeing, which is necessary to open the door to Level 5. Executives who are satisfied with Level 4 run the risk of becoming "fossils" or "relics" in their organizations. When they stop listening to others and stop learning, they stop growing as leaders.

Level 5: The Elusive Peak

Research shows that more than eighty percent of us will stop growing at Level 4 or before. This statistic explains why people we think of as truly wise are relatively rare. Yet ultimately, those who continue to grow toward Level 5 will begin to see the limitations of even their own Level 4, self-authored paradigm as it, too, is challenged and contradicted over time. Although there are notable exceptions, most people who make it to this point are in their sixties or older.

If we continue to do the tough work of Vertical development, a new Level 5 lens will eventually emerge. This final lens, like the ones before it, will allow us to have an even clearer understanding of the world than the previous lenses allowed. A Level 5 lens enables us to organize all the information we have gained through our previous lenses. This new organizing filter will view the world, others, and self through a universal, higher-order set of values or principles, including honesty, integrity, being open to and valuing others, and courage.

Level 5 thinking goes beyond what is best for me and considers what is best for the community and the world. These values are still self-authored (Inside-Out) because we deal internally with the challenges that contradict our Level 4 understanding. At Level 5 we understand that something bigger than just our paradigm needs to hold all of the different possible paradigms together. That is the role of the higher-order values that will become our new, final lens.

In meeting with others in an organization, a Level 5 leader is thinking how to contribute to a much larger set of goals. The Level 5 leader isn't driven to personally benefit (like Level 2 leaders), or trying to be respected in the eyes of others (like Level 3 leaders), or worried about achieving the goal (like Level 4 leaders). At Level 5, she knows the best answer to the problem doesn't lie within her, but within the people in the room. The challenge is to extract it from the people around the table.

Robert Frost wrote, "We all sit around in a ring and suppose, while the secret sits in the center and knows." This is a profound and rare observation. It's what makes Level 5 people so effective as they lead in the most complex circumstances.

Your Rate of Progress

This chapter has provided just a skeleton outline about the various levels of leadership. No doubt you have questions, but the following chapters will be increasingly specific and will put some meat on these bones. But before we dive more deeply into each level, let's talk briefly about the normal pace of Vertical growth and what you can do to accelerate it.

It takes longer and longer to move from level to level the farther you go on your Vertical journey. Just as our bodies grow faster in childhood, our Vertical development is more rapid in the early stages.

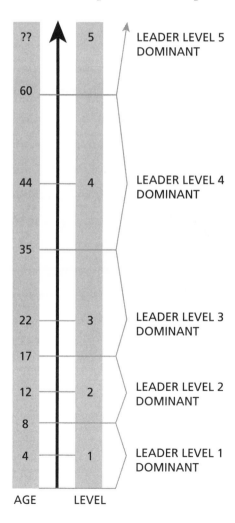

We have identified the average range of ages for each of the levels, but an individual might vary considerably from the average. Too many factors are in play (including family upbringing, unforeseen circumstances, and experiences of challenge and change) to allow us to be more specific.

Research reveals many examples of people who have arrested their development, or stopped growing prematurely. Eight to ten percent of adults stop growing at Level 2. Other people reach levels of Vertical development at ages earlier than expected. For example, some teenagers suffer the challenge and contradiction of life-threatening illnesses and through their difficulties gain an Inside-Out, Level 4 understanding that gives them wisdom far beyond their years.

Based on numerous historical accounts, we see that leaders such as Abraham Lincoln, Mahatma Gandhi, Martin Luther King, Jr., and Mother Teresa changed the world less from what they knew (Lateral development) than from their measurably higher maturity of perspective (Vertical development). Each had peers who were arguably more educated and well versed in their respective fields of influence, but what enabled each of them to change the world was their ability to rise above the challenges of their circumstance and see the big picture in a way that displayed a higher level of Vertical understanding.

When we evaluate Martin Luther King, Jr.'s first-person writings, it appears that by the time of his assassination at age thirty-nine he understood the world in a Level 5 way—decades earlier than would be expected based on his age alone. It seems that Abraham Lincoln moved from Level 4 toward Level 5 during the last two years of the Civil War at age fifty-six, also somewhat ahead of the norm. Gandhi appears to have developed at a more normal pace and became Level 5 by his mid-sixties. Mother Teresa was thirty-eight when she left behind a relatively secure and comfortable job as headmistress in a Calcutta convent school to work and live among the poorest and most desperate people of the city. It is no coincidence that all of these exceptional leaders faced extreme challenges and contradictions to the way they saw their world. But it is very likely those same challenges propelled them to the highest levels of Vertical development.

> Becoming a Level 5 leader doesn't require sacrificing your life, but it requires sacrificing your current lens. You have to see challenges as opportunities for growth—for yourself and for those you lead.

More than the mere passage of time, persevering through challenging experiences that contradict our current understanding is what promotes growth. Therefore, the good news is that we can accelerate Vertical growth by identifying and intentionally leaning into even the smallest challenges. In doing so we move forward intentionally, rather than having our growth determined by the whims of circumstance. And we can better control our developmental progress *if we know the Map.*

My friend Mark and I drove through a lot of cities and remote areas that were new to us as we went across the country. It was tempting to stop and explore many of those sights we had never seen. But that Rand McNally map on the dashboard kept showing us how far we still needed to go to get to our Promised Land.

Similarly, it's easy to get stalled along one's life journey for any number of reasons. And while much can be said for Lateral growth along the way, it is no substitute for the opportunity to develop a lens that will make you the best possible leader you can be. Knowing the Map will make it easier for you to make your Vertical journey more efficiently and effectively.

Consider this . . .

1. Who are the leaders you admire most? Why?

2. In your own words, how would you describe the difference between Lateral growth and Vertical growth?

3. In what ways are you currently attempting to grow Laterally? Do you have an inclination yet of what more you could do that would result in Vertical growth as well?

4. In your life so far, what challenging situations can you recall that have contributed to your Vertical growth?

5. As you briefly examined the five levels in this chapter, at what point on the Map would you insert a pin signifying "You are here"? What factors and characteristics led you to this conclusion?

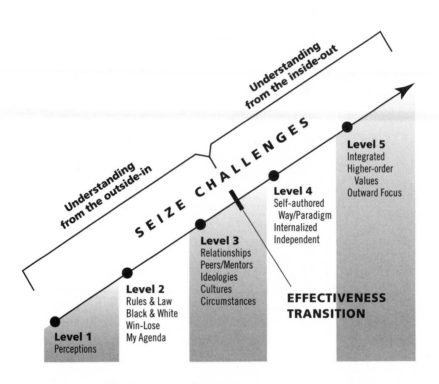

Understanding from the outside-in

Understanding from the inside-out

SEIZE CHALLENGES

Level 1
Perceptions

Level 2
Rules & Law
Black & White
Win-Lose
My Agenda

Level 3
Relationships
Peers/Mentors
Ideologies
Cultures
Circumstances

Level 4
Self-authored
Way/Paradigm
Internalized
Independent

Level 5
Integrated
Higher-order
Values
Outward Focus

**EFFECTIVENESS
TRANSITION**

Section Two

ON THE ROAD

The first two chapters presented an overview of our life journeys, taking a high-level look at Vertical development. They were the 30,000-foot view to provide a big-picture perspective of the Map. The next four chapters are a ground-level examination of the characteristics of each of the primary mileposts along the way. Every level of adult development is like arriving at a different city with its own distinctions and new insights.

If you aren't very far along on the road of Vertical development, much of this will be new to you. Even if you have traveled far on instinct alone, these chapters should help you understand the progress you have made. Just as importantly, you will get a better comprehension of the people you are leading at various stages of development. You will learn how to identify where they are, understand why some of them seem to be stuck and unable to grow further, and discover what drives and motivates leaders at the different levels.

Each chapter in this section will include a brief summary of a much more intensive interview with a business leader at each level of development. After providing a general description of each level, it can be helpful to see what someone at that level looks like in a leadership position.

[NOTE: I have only summarized interviews with four leaders in the following chapters: Stan in Chapter 3 (Level 2), Joe in Chapter 4 (Level 3), Kate in Chapter 5 (Level 4), and Henry in Chapter 6 (Level 5). If you would like to see the full interviews, they are available at www.LeadersLyceum.com/MAP.]

As we've seen, Level 1 is the stage of early childhood development, so because everyone reading the book has passed that stage, we will spend our time on the road between Level 2 and Level 5. Keep in mind that you don't instantly jump from one level to the next higher one. Your vehicle takes you gradually from your existing level to the next one, and there's a lot of real estate in between. The city you just left will continue to fade as you approach the influence of the next one.

In Section 3 we will go into even greater detail about moving from point to point. For now, however, simply try to familiarize yourself with the various levels. Refer to the diagrams at the beginning of these chapters so you won't forget where you are heading.

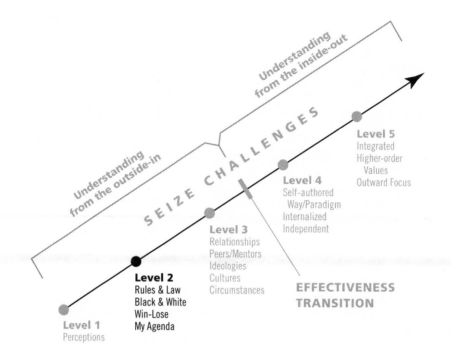

Understanding from the outside-in

Understanding from the inside-out

SEIZE CHALLENGES

EFFECTIVENESS TRANSITION

Level 1
Perceptions

Level 2
Rules & Law
Black & White
Win-Lose
My Agenda

Level 3
Relationships
Peers/Mentors
Ideologies
Cultures
Circumstances

Level 4
Self-authored
Way/Paradigm
Internalized
Independent

Level 5
Integrated
Higher-order
Values
Outward Focus

Chapter 3

LEVEL 2: IT'S ALL ABOUT ME

If you have, or have had, a middle-school child, you no doubt have encountered the Level 2 stage of Vertical development. The child has moved through the perception-is-reality bubble of Level 1 and has arrived at some rather emphatic beliefs about life. At Level 2, the child sees the world in black and white, with little room for shades of gray. People and problems are judged as right or wrong, good or bad, nice or mean. And since the child is the one doing the judging, the problem is almost always with the other person. It's human nature to blame others . . . at least at this stage.

A Look at the World through a Me-First Lens

When my third child, JT, was in middle school, he was in a running battle with a girl from his class whom we will call Amy. The situation had gotten to the point where he had been talked to several times before we found out about it and were called to the principal's office for the dreaded parent meeting. When JT was asked to share what was going on, his response was that Amy was *always* mean to him and that he was *always* nice to her.

At the time, JT wasn't able to understand himself as a person who sometimes says nice things and sometimes says mean things. He saw himself as a victim of circumstance where he was losing, and it wasn't fair. His inability to take ownership for the role he played in the conflict is what Outside-In understanding looks like at Level 2.

While I wasn't thrilled with JT's behavior, I understood it to be "normal" for his age. I used the opportunity to try to explain to him what he didn't yet know—that Amy had a perspective as well, and that it would have been preferable for him to try to understand or even empathize with her feelings. This approach had the potential to help him shape what would become movement toward a Level 3 understanding of himself and others. However, because he was still at Level 2 where rewards and consequences were what motivated his behavior, I gave him consequences he wouldn't soon forget. He was grounded at home in addition to an in-school punishment, and we gave him a whole new series of chores to lock in the idea that he would "lose" again if he chose a similar set of behaviors.

Interestingly, at about the same time one teacher told us that the "meanness" little boys and girls learn in elementary school is perfected by middle school. It makes perfect sense because children, on average, become fully Level 2 at around twelve years of age. At this level of development they see themselves in simple, categorical ways. They perceive their own way of thinking as the best, so they gravitate to a like-minded crowd and then ostracize those who are different in a win/lose battle of existence. In the Level 2 mind, if two different categories of people coexist, they both can't be right—if one is right, then the other by definition must be wrong.

By the time most students are in high school, they begin to not only tolerate various opinions, but eventually they may even celebrate the differences that previously separated them. Those who maintain the "I'm right, and therefore you're wrong" understanding are perceived as immature and become the outcasts rather than the judges. A Level 2 mentality isn't pretty in high school students.

Even worse, we sometimes find adults who have parked their vehicles at Level 2 and settled in for an extended stay. We experience them as broken, and we are less tolerant of the behaviors associated with their concrete, black and white, me-first understanding. It is expected that most individuals will be fully Level 3 by their early twenties, and even those who are a little behind the curve should get to that level by their late twenties.

The ability to understand another's position—whether "the other" is an individual or an organization—is a place of understanding that those at Level 2 cannot yet go. When I asked JT, "Can't you put yourself in Amy's shoes?" he responded with a blank stare. I was asking him to go to a place beyond his capacity to understand. But when you ask the same question and get the same blank stare from a Level 2 adult whose development is arrested, it's no longer tolerable, cute, or excusable.

The Level 2 view of the world is an Outside-In, concrete, black-and-white understanding of things and circumstances. Everything is viewed in simple, categorical terms. The understanding of conflict is an either/or dichotomy, like one team pitted against the other on the playing field. The options are win, lose, or draw, and Level 2 individuals always strive to win. The idea of compromise or achieving a win-win solution exceeds this understanding.

Indeed, the drive to win determines the extent to which Level 2 individuals will abide by the rules. If the reward for obedience is big enough, or the consequence of breaking the rules severe enough, then compliance will seem like what is best at the time. But if the assessment is made that more could be gained by breaking the rules, a decision might be made to steal, for instance, whether it be office supplies, time, money, or even feelings of self-respect from another. These are the results of someone with an amoral balance sheet.

Not surprisingly, the prison population has a disproportionate number of Level 2 individuals. Psychologists often diagnose these people as sociopaths, simply defined as those who don't understand, acknowledge, or participate in the norms of society. They usually have a complete disregard for the rights of others and an overinflated sense of themselves. When Level 2 prisoners are asked about their crimes, no matter how heinous, they consistently justify their actions as what they believed to be best thing they could do for themselves at the time.[19]

When Level 2 adults find themselves in the workplace rather than the prison system, the circumstances surrounding the "crime" may be more palatable, but their understanding of the world isn't. Remember that they have not outgrown their "me first" attitude and are still totally unable to see more than two sides—my side and the wrong side. One side must win and the other must lose, with no possibility of compromise or resolution between the two. Therefore, they feel little compunction over cheating on an expense report, lying about or demeaning a coworker for their own gain, or stealing from the organization or a client in some way if the benefit to them outweighs the consequence.

How Level 2 People See Themselves

Self-interest is the lens through which Level 2 individuals view themselves. They have much to say about *me*, but very little about *we*. In addition to being overly egocentric, a Level 2 understanding is strictly categorical: I'm a winner; I'm athletic; I'm intelligent; I'm a hard worker; I'm your manager; I'm the man of this house; I'm your mother. The category is crisp, concise, and sure. You are no more likely to hear Level 2 individuals describe themselves in complex terms than you are to hear a nuanced self-assessment from a ten-year-old. They haven't yet internalized their perceptions, and are the most Outside-In of the adult levels.

> A friend was telling me about having dinner at a restaurant where two women were at the neighboring table. One woman was doing literally all the talking. In the hour he was there, her companion hardly got to say a word as the talkative one moved from her health problems, to a conflict at the garage where she had to take her car, to family disagreements, and back to other health problems. The woman was still rattling on when he left. He said he was tempted to lean over and at least see if the second woman was capable of verbal speech.

You know people like this. Think about the adult family member who only thinks of himself and the way any decision is going to impact him and only him, and who can't seem to see things through the eyes of others. Think about the coworker or boss who only sees her own perspective and dogmatically criticizes anyone else's opinions. Think about people who are defined by overly simplistic, dogmatic ideologies, who believe that they must prevail against those who think differently. All are examples of middle-schoolers in adult bodies, except they do their bullying not on the playground, but at Thanksgiving dinner, during the annual performance review, with a bullhorn, or worse.

One of the remarkable stories of the last decades took place prior to the 1994 winter Olympic games. You may not remember much about what happened in Lillehammer, Norway, but if you were old enough, you probably remember the name of ice skater Tonya Harding.

I don't profess to speak with authority on Harding's thoughts or motives, yet I can say that her actions are indicative of an adult stalled at Level 2. Harding's career was plagued by a series of "crises" that occurred too often to be coincidental. She was late for events because she was stranded in traffic. She asked to restart a skating program if her dress came unhooked or her skate blade was loose. She claimed at one point to be suffering from an ovarian cyst that was in danger of bursting, and prior to an event in 1993 the competition organizers received an anonymous threat which excluded her from the qualification round. One medal ceremony was delayed when she couldn't be found, and she was allowed to restart a free skate after missing the opening jump because she said her bootlace was too short. Harding went through multiple coaching changes, and she frequently made it known that she suffered from asthma, even though she was known to smoke occasionally.

But the event that made Tonya Harding a household name came at the 1994 U.S. Figure Skating Championships—the qualifier for the Olympics. Harding's main competitor at the time was Nancy Kerrigan. Harding's ex-husband and a bodyguard allegedly hired a third man to break Kerrigan's right leg with a collapsible police baton. The attack failed to break Kerrigan's leg, but bruised it severely enough that Kerrigan was forced to withdraw. Consequently, Harding won the event.

Harding eventually confessed to covering up the attack but threatened to take legal action if not allowed to skate in the Olympics. Kerrigan, fully recovered by then, took the silver medal with Harding finishing eighth. Harding avoided jail time by pleading guilty to hindering the investigation, but in turn was stripped of her U.S. Figure Skating Championship win and banned from further competition for life. While Harding has maintained her innocence, the other three conspirators have not. Harding's ex-husband, her bodyguard, and the attacker all testified against Harding as part of their own plea bargain.[20]

In this story, perhaps we get a view into the understanding of a Level 2 mind. The egocentric, win/lose mentality leads Level 2 people to act in ways that only consider what is best for themselves at the time. They are unable to see the world from another's perspective, and often act in ways that are destructive to the larger communities of which they are a part.

We had an engagement with a company that faced significant problems, largely due to the disruptive nature of a Level 2 executive. The man was brilliantly creative but destructive in his relationships among the executive team and his direct reports. Problems arose because everything was about him: his needs, his work, his bonus, his strategy for the company. His leadership philosophy, in his own words, was, "You either outwork people or you steamroll over them; there is really no other way." There was no perspective other than his own "me first" one to draw from. You were either with him or against him, and this led to his creating wedges between people and ultimately forcing them to choose sides. A climate of stress and fear pervaded his direct reports, and stories circulated among the whole organization about his behavior and threatened what was once a highly productive organizational culture. The shadow from the Level 2 leader can be quite long and very destructive. A defining moment for organizations that employ Level 2 leaders in executive roles is the decision whether their unique talents and contributions outweigh their capacity for destruction.

How Level 2 People See Others

Since Level 2 people see themselves in neat, simple categories, they see others in that same categorical way (nice, mean, smart, etc.). Level 2s always look out for their own good, and they presume others use the same lens of self-interest, creating an ongoing sense of suspicion toward everyone with whom they interact. The only options they can see for any situation are win, lose, or draw, and they think everyone else feels the same way.

The leadership philosophy of the Level 2 adult is, "You scratch my back; I'll scratch yours." It is a quid pro quo mentality that does not take into account that some people may, at least in part, be motivated by things other than personal gain. If you tell Level 2 people your motivation for being involved in a certain project is to help others, to serve the client well, to make a difference in the world, or to be a part of something bigger than yourself, they won't believe you. Your real motivation, they will believe based on their own not-yet-developed value system, is based in what you get out of it personally, or at the least because it makes you feel good.

When Level 2 people aren't in charge, their mentality is, "Tell me the rules, and I'll play your game if I get what I want." This mentality is again an exchange-oriented way of understanding the world. Today's marketplace and organizations value open communication, creative thinking, and the leveraging of differences for more effective decisions. In such settings, Level 2 employees can have devastating effects on the productivity and effectiveness that will lead to success.

> I once coached an executive and asked him what was most important in leading others. He said that teamwork was most important to him. I thought to myself, *Good response*, and then I asked him *why* teamwork was so important to him. His surprising answer was that teamwork is important because it helps him get his way! I am sure his definition of teamwork does not show up in any dictionary. The point is that it's not what people say that is most important, but rather the level from which they are speaking. It was my probing of his concept of teamwork that revealed his Level 2-ness.

The Level 2's drive to come out ahead in any exchange doesn't bode well for romance or other satisfying adult friendships. Such people have an oversimplified understanding of rich and complex relationships—one that's very categorical and exchange oriented. Remember, they are stuck in the me-first mentality of middle-schoolers. Roles in their relationships are very narrowly defined: I am the breadwinner, you take care of the house; I make the decisions, you follow my lead; I am the dad, you are the child; etc. When relationships go smoothly (defined as everyone playing their roles "the right way"), the Level 2 person is winning. But any discord or threat to the expected balances of power is perceived as a loss, and a Level 2's extraordinary efforts not to lose can include verbal or even physical abuse.

In a marital relationship, Level 2 spouses can create a great deal of instability and dysfunction. If their self-interests happen to align with the interests of the marriage or with those of the other spouse, they can appear strong, smart, and protective. But when a spouse's positions differ, somebody has to win and somebody has to lose—there's no such thing as compromise. When Level 2 spouses are in a position of financial or physical authority, they almost always win.

The longer adults maintain a Level 2 mindset, the more difficult it becomes to resolve the inappropriateness of their behavior. It is hard to send another grownup to timeout—especially if he or she is your boss or spouse! When we find ourselves under the authority of Level 2 leaders, it can be very painful. Yet when worse comes to worse, the option is always open to exit a place of employment. In a romantic relationship, however, disengagement or divorce is difficult and sometimes dangerous because more than likely it will be viewed as the ultimate loss by the Level 2 spouse.

Mark Twain wrote rather facetiously, "In all matters of opinion, our adversaries are insane," but this statement is a reasonably accurate description of the thinking of adults at Level 2.

The Level 2 Leader

Research shows that Level 2 professionals over the age of thirty comprise less than ten percent of the highly educated, professional, adult population.[21] The good news is that is fewer than about one in every ten people we meet each day. The bad news? That's almost one in every ten people! And when we encounter one of those Level 2 adults in a leadership role (bosses, teachers, church leaders, etc.), it is somewhat unnerving, certainly frustrating, and can even be a little scary.

How do Level 2 leaders rise to positions of authority? Some are the founding entrepreneurs of an organization that has been successful. As long as these people are in charge (winning), things can go fairly smoothly. But when tension in the business or conflict with others arises, the limited capacity of the Level 2 leader's understanding will come to light. The driving desire to win combined with the Outside-In emphasis may work in the person's favor—but usually only temporarily. Level 2 employees can make great strides in Lateral growth, which is often noticed and rewarded by supervisors for a while. Level 2 leaders often have high intelligence or great expertise, but eventually it becomes evident that such positive attributes are no substitute for Vertical development.

Stan is a forty-three-year-old mid-level vice president who has worked for twenty years at a company we will call Textile Products, Inc. TPI is the largest manufacturer in its industry and best in its class, generating over $7 billion in revenue. I had asked TPI's CEO if I could interview someone in the organization who had appeared to have great capacity for leadership early in his or her career, yet had not risen to meet that potential. The CEO realized something was holding Stan back, but he couldn't put his finger on the exact cause.

The reason I wanted to interview corporate executives was because I had sat through many talent evaluation meetings where the team choosing next-generation leaders couldn't say exactly why they lacked confidence in certain people who seemed to have promise. Too often they wrote it off to the "Peter Principle," the long-standing maxim that in an organizational hierarchy, every employee tends to rise to his or her level of incompetence. Based on the 1969 book, the principle suggests that people who do things well continue to get rewarded with promotions, but each promotion brings a demand for new skills and responsibilities. Eventually the employees find themselves doing work that is neither satisfying nor productive.[22]

It was my intent to interview enough high-level managers to show that the underlying problem was not so much the Peter Principle as it was the inability to continue his or her Vertical development—to make the crucial transition from Level 2 to Level 3, and then beyond. Only then can they move from an Outside-In understanding of the world and begin to develop their own Inside-Out comprehension. (We have conducted hundreds of such interviews, and will select a sample to demonstrate each of the levels as we go along.)

Stan appeared uneasy and a little skeptical of our time together, sitting forward in his chair and speaking with some intensity. At first I was impressed with his quickness and the certainty with which he responded to my questions. In fact, my initial reading was that he was Level 4, which would have been a reasonable expectation based on his age and position.

It soon became apparent, however, that he didn't understand the world, himself, or others from Level 4. What initially came across as confidence and certainty quickly degenerated to narcissism, concreteness, and simplicity. He had great difficulty describing the complex relationship between differing points of view. He viewed almost everything through the lens of "What's in it for me?" In his win-or-lose world all motivation to work, and work well, was about personal gain or loss, which he assumed motivated everyone else as well.

> Level 2 leaders are extremely simple and concrete in their understanding of the world. They don't merely make the complex simple; they oversimplify complexity to ludicrous and potentially dangerous extremes.

Stan's black-and-white, overly simplistic, either/or understanding of the world was evident throughout the interview. For example, he said there are only two reasons for hierarchy in organizations: to resolve conflicts between opposing points of view and for outsiders who need to understand the structure. While decision-making and structure are certainly two reasons for corporate hierarchy, they are by no means the only two. Dozens of reasons exist, good and bad, and they interact in ways that increase the complexity of the hierarchy's purpose to the point that volumes of books have been written on the subject.

If a supervisor chose someone else's idea rather than his, Stan didn't concede that the other way might be better, only that two equally valid opinions had been presented and the company had gone with the other one. Still, he saw such decisions as a personal loss, and he admitted that he hated to lose.

In the interview, I posed a scenario where everyone was trying to get from one town to another, with alternate routes possible, and others had simply asked Stan to come along with them on a route different from the one he had suggested. I asked, "What impact would that have on you?" He responded, "It's a loss. I don't like to lose. I didn't do the job I should have done to convince my manager that my way was a better way. So I take it personally."

As we continued our conversation, I asked him, "Why is not losing so important to you?" He was brutally honest: "I don't know. I don't like to lose at anything. I've been beating my son at board games since he was four years old, and he knew I would beat him until he was smart enough to beat me."

His personal goal was to figure out easier and quicker ways to get things done—not to improve profit margins or move on to bigger prospects. His motivation? "I just want to get this stuff over with so I can go home." The interview also showed that Stan believed everyone else makes sense of the world the way he does. Think of the more than forty people reporting to him in his procurement group. What do you think work life was like for them?

What if *everyone* you came in contact with viewed you as a competitor who impedes their primary motivation of getting what they want and making their lives simpler? Imagine living in such a world.

The interview with Stan started to get a little uncomfortable toward the end. He was capable of telling me what he did, but grew frustrated when I pushed him to explain more of *how he understood what he did.* As the interviewer, I actually did what most people do with Level 2 leaders—I gave him an out that felt like a win, diffused the tension, and complimented him even when I didn't really mean it.

These are the strategies we all use to deal with the destructive, manipulative, immature responses of Level 2 leaders. Sending them to "timeout" isn't usually within our authority, even though that's what we would do with a middle-schooler who acted like Stan.

Don't misunderstand: Stan's limitations as a leader have nothing to do with intelligence or training. He has acquired the knowledge, skills, and abilities required to perform his job. (In other words, his Lateral development met the company's expectations.) Still, the CEO's instincts about Stan were accurate. Because Stan's Vertical development had stalled at Level 2, he didn't meet the expectations required for leadership advancement that would continue his ascent in the organization.

One of the big mistakes we make in our organizations—and it happens frequently—is promoting our best salesperson, best technician, or best accountant. In other words, we promote the people with the best Lateral development skills. It's quite natural, but shortsighted, to advance the people we trust with our technical questions. We promote them, but then we're shocked to discover they can't lead a team! They don't have adequate Vertical development. This observation is especially common in younger employees who statistically are more likely to be at lower leader levels. For this reason, growing young leaders in their Vertical development should be a priority for organizations.

Accentuating Lateral development is the way a Level 2 leader survives. People of above-average intelligence, like Stan, learn the vocabulary of their organization, industry, or community. They take advantage of their education, gain expertise over time, and often get by or even seem to excel at their jobs. But imagine what it must be like to be Stan, dealing with complexity coming from every direction, and holding it together by simplifying everything down to the most concrete and elementary components. What must it be like to try to hold those components together in a way where others don't find you out?

Even Stan's understanding of himself is simplistic and categorical. Level 2 individuals see themselves as people who always have to win. For Stan to move to Level 3, he must begin to put himself in other people's shoes and maybe even see the benefit in sometimes letting them win (not least of all the four-year-olds with whom he plays board games). The concreteness of his understanding will have to be challenged in a way that lets him see that there are hypothetical possibilities, compromises, and synergistic solutions to his problems. There will be more gray in his vocabulary.

As a forty-three-year-old leader of a department, someone Stan's age and position ought to be at least moving in the direction of Level 4, but first he will need to develop to Level 3. Is there hope for him at this stage of his life? Yes, but it won't be easy. Development never is, but the longer you stay arrested at any level, the more the difficulty gets multiplied. I often think of developmental change being analogous to wading through concrete. When concrete is first poured, you can walk through it as long as you make a little effort and keep moving. However, the longer you stay in one place (arrest your development), the more the concrete hardens. And the harder the concrete, the bigger the hammer of challenge is needed to break out and resume the growth that should have taken place years or even (as in Stan's case) decades before. Before Stan moves on to Level 3, he will need to face a challenge so big that not doing the tough work of developing will be seen as a bigger loss than just continuing to cram the challenge into his existing, self-centered, oversimplified categories.

Level 2 isn't necessarily a black hole for anyone. All of us experienced this stage when we were younger. Through an awkward and often difficult road, we learned enough to move forward into Level 3. For adults whose development is arrested in Level 2, the same process still applies: learning from trial and error, gaining insight from a trusted mentor, and discovering that people have inherent value—they're not all competitors!

If you've moved beyond Level 2, it may be instructive and encouraging to look back at that stage of your life. Can you remember a difficult circumstance from your teenage years that gave you a more mature understanding of life? The new or better perspective—the new lens you gained through those experiences—is an example of Vertical growth.

Moving On

Does Stan's story sound familiar? It should. Anyone who is higher than Level 2 necessarily went through that stage of development earlier in life, so you might recognize the description as part of your past. It is a previous lens you are *now* able to take a perspective on, even though at the time it was simply the way the world made sense to you. Like looking back on a trail map to understand ground already covered, you can gain perspective on where you currently are and how far you have yet to go.

A recent coaching client told me of an extraordinary experience he had as a young man that signaled his growth from Level 2 to Level 3. During his senior year in college as a member of ROTC he participated in a camp exercise where all the cadets were evaluated on their various skill sets in outdoor leadership activities. He saw himself as a good leader, and when the results were posted he had scored first in each of the twelve leadership exercises. Much to his surprise, his final grade for the camp was only an 83. The following day he met with the commanding officer and asked why his overall grade was so low. The commander looked straight into his eyes and calmly asked, "When achieving those scores, who did you help along the way?" My coaching client, now in his late forties, said it was the most impactful thing anyone has said to him. "At that moment I knew my life had changed; I was never going to be the leader I wanted to be if I did not bring others with me."

As executive coaches we hear these kinds of developmental epiphanies frequently. Each story is unique but has profound meaning for its author. I wish we could bottle such insight and give it to a client who is struggling at a lower leader level. All we can say for sure is that timing or readiness to hear the message is everything. I am pretty sure the cadet could not have heard the wisdom of his officer years or maybe even months earlier. There is a good chance he would have found a way to ignore, dismiss, or resist the advice—not because he was not listening, but because he was not ready to hear the wisdom.

I notice myself repeating things to my children that my parents said to me—things I pledged that I would never say. So the only insight I can provide to these mysteries is that developmental readiness and an openness to learning something new about yourself is critical. I remind myself to stay open and to allow the poke, prod, nudge, and probe of challenges to provide gateways to a new level of awareness.

As we will see in the following chapters, every level has its blind spots. One of the biggest blind spots at Level 2 is an inability to empathize with others. Level 2 leaders can understand that someone else's position is different from theirs, but they don't realize that isn't the same as actually understanding the different position. They can't put themselves in others' shoes. They can't suspend their own agendas in a way that allows them to coordinate it with the agendas of others. Such limited understanding is a far cry from what is needed to solve the complex issues facing us in all our roles—at work, at home, and in our personal lives.

When we encounter adults at Level 2, we may make an incorrect, or incomplete, prognosis: "He's such a tool;" "It's always all about her;" "He lives in his own self-centered little world." Such assessments may be true. Then again, it may be that the person is seeing an adult world through the lens of a middle-schooler. It's understandable that confusion would result.

Chris Evert is a Hall of Fame tennis professional. After reading the autobiography of a younger tennis star, Andre Agassi, she empathized with what he was going through in a way she couldn't understand or express when she was his age. She wrote,

Consider the life of a tennis phenom. From age 15 until about 30, we're put into an abnormal and potentially destructive environment. We have people working for us, complimenting our every move and catering to our needs. We're never accountable for wayward behavior. It could be

something as insignificant as getting out of a speeding ticket with an autograph. The important life lessons most people learn during this time are put on hold. We don't learn survival skills such as independence and personal responsibility, and it catches up with us. You go from being a kid to an adult without doing any significant maturing. That's why I have empathy for what Andre is going through.[23]

From her more mature perspective, Evert saw the "bubble" Agassi experienced because of his fame and fortune. He was so protected that he didn't learn the lessons most people learn. With the benefit of her age and experience, Evert saw the truth and it moved her with compassion.

In the same way, but perhaps not to the same extent, many parents are like those who shielded Agassi: they try to protect their children from the consequences of their choices. They prevent them from experiencing the challenges and contradictions that force them to grow. These parents may mean well and love their children, but they risk robbing their kids of opportunities to grow and mature.

Adult growth toward Level 3 can begin when Level 2s discover their personal agendas actually limit their success and that coordinating with others' agendas is actually the bigger win . . . when they realize putting themselves in others' shoes facilitates more beneficial relationships . . . when they begin to see themselves as connected to, not just different from, others and their perspectives. As they gradually let go of their win-or-lose, self-protective attitudes and start interacting with others, the Vertical journey usually results in greater effectiveness and success. The Level 3 understanding is a welcome relief, and that is where we now turn.

Consider This . . .

1. As you read the description of Level 2 thinking (those who literally can't understand other people's perspectives, can't stand to lose, see everything through a lens of personal gain or loss, etc.), who are some people who immediately came to mind? Why?

2. Why are Level 2 adults sometimes perceived to be more "together" than they really are?

3. What are some problematic behaviors of Level 2 adults you have noticed in the context of:

    Personal relationships?

    Workplace encounters?

    Romantic relationships?

    Social or religious affiliations?

4. Can you identify a particular challenge or specific time in your past when you realized you needed to leave behind your Level 2 lens and move on with your Vertical growth? What prompted the insight and growth?

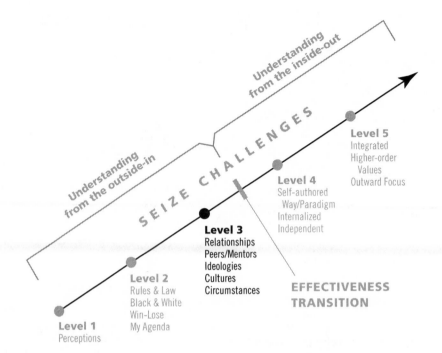

Understanding from the outside-in

Understanding from the inside-out

SEIZE CHALLENGES

Level 5
Integrated
Higher-order
Values
Outward Focus

Level 4
Self-authored
Way/Paradigm
Internalized
Independent

Level 3
Relationships
Peers/Mentors
Ideologies
Cultures
Circumstances

**EFFECTIVENESS
TRANSITION**

Level 2
Rules & Law
Black & White
Win-Lose
My Agenda

Level 1
Perceptions

Chapter 4

LEVEL 3:
OVERWHELMED BY
OUTSIDE INFLUENCES

It turns out that Sally isn't always nice, Billy isn't always mean, and Tommy is more than simply athletic. In retrospect, that seems to go without saying. But for those entrenched at Level 2, this is breaking news! It takes a while to acknowledge the many complexities of life and continue the journey toward Level 3. And as we do, we discover that we need some help.

The challenges and contradictions that dislodge Level 2 understanding—whether on the playground or in the boardroom—show that the world is not as black-and-white as once thought. As we move toward Level 3, the clear-cut, win-or-lose order of the world gives way to a grayer, more hypothetical, more compromising, yet more connected way of understanding things. Those developmental disruptions allow us to see the chinks in the armor of our Level 2 understanding.

Exactly what causes those developmental disruptions at this stage of Vertical growth? We start hearing a lot of other voices in our worlds—many of which challenge our simplistic way of thinking. For a while we try to filter all those comments through the either/or mindset, keeping as much as possible in black or white categories for as long as possible—sometimes for far too long. Yet most of us eventually realize we need to reconsider how we see ourselves, others, and the world.

Initially, losing the certainty of Level 2 understanding causes a lack of stability. Although we can see that the order of our world is less concrete than we thought, we are not yet able to decide for ourselves what the new order should be. To regain our stability, we will need help from outside influences.

> There is a sense of losing our footing—our stability—every time we grow Vertically. At every level of growth, we must give up or let go of our current lens to gain a new and better one. While loosening our grip is never easy, it's necessary to keep growing.

The Power of Peer Pressure

In the early stages of development toward Level 3, which typically begin in the early teens, we increasingly let go of the understanding that characterized our Level 2 world. Because parents are the primary shapers of understanding at Level 2 for most of us, we tend to discard their influence as we begin to move toward a Level 3 understanding. Yet even though we may initially decide that parental influence is irrelevant, we still require outside sources to help us shape our new understanding.

During our teen years, the next most readily available source of advice (after parents) is the people we trust the most—our friends. In simple terms, we call this *peer pressure*, a powerful social force that compels us to go along with what our peers think makes sense. Peer pressure can be positive or negative. In either case, it is our gradually emerging Level 3 response to this pressure that defines our dependence on outside sources to help us understand our world.

Social media (including Facebook, Twitter, Instagram, and many others) play into the need to be known, liked, accepted, and included. While such tools can be used effectively from any level, people at Level 3 often are absorbed in these pursuits, which simultaneously provide a window and a mirror for them to understand and be understood. Quite often, the reactions of others to a post or tweet—or more disconcerting, the lack of reaction—let them know whether they are valued or not, included or not, popular or not, pretty or not, crazy or not. And these factors are always measured against the scale of how many "likes" the person has gotten compared to friends and acquaintances.

When we talk to these teenagers and young adults—or better yet, when we simply watch their responses to posts—we realize they don't merely *have* Twitter posts, they *are* their Twitter posts. Their whole identity is defined by the responses they receive. Most of us understand this Outside-In-ness as normal and age-appropriate for Level 3. However, if you have middle-aged friends or family members who still get their identity from their profiles, their status, or their "walls," it seems a little weird and kind of sad. I've seen Level 4, Inside-Out people use social media very effectively, so the fact that you might be a Facebook user doesn't automatically make you Level 3. But if you're in your forties and you use social media to feel good about who you are, it might be time for some self-reflection.

> The key to growth beyond Level 3 isn't dependence on an outside source; it's how you understand and interpret the sources of input that give you insight. Yes, social networking is fun and important, but does it define you? Are you upset when your posts don't get recognized?

One more point on peer pressure: all of us know the potential dangers of succumbing to pressure from the wrong people based on our own earlier experiences in life as well as observing it in the lives of others. Teenagers have a natural inclination to fit in with peers, a reality which prompts many parents to make a point of knowing who their kids' friends are. What those friends do and the kinds of decisions they make have powerful influence on each other, and parents are right to be concerned. It's likely that your mother asked you the same question my mother used to ask me: "If all your friends decided to jump off a cliff, would you jump, too?"

> A note to parents: You may feel that your repeated attempts to discuss the dangers of peer pressure with your children are like talking to a fencepost, yet you have more influence than you realize. Many young adults who grow up

in healthy, loving households go away to college where, in retrospect, their parents miraculously become a whole lot smarter! As your "young adults" eventually see the wisdom in what you have taught them, they tend to give greater weight to what you have to say. It's encouraging that many college seniors identify one of their parents as the leader who has most positively influenced them. It gives hope to those of us in the throes of parenting teenagers that our influence in their lives may not be lost to the degree we've feared.

The transition from Level 2 to Level 3 is not easy, linear, or immediate. That period of growth stretches across a decade or more, so our teenage years will be split between the two levels. For young teenagers, having their agenda satisfied (Level 2) may still be more dominant than the influence of others (Level 3), so if they fear they will get in trouble for submitting to peer pressure, they may choose to not go along. If, however, potential negative consequences don't outweigh the feeling of connection they believe they'll gain by going along with peers, then they're much more likely to cave in under pressure by their friends. Parents should never underestimate the wicked cocktail created when children mix wanting to get their way with the outside influence of their peers. They are both "winning" (getting their way) and being defined by their friends when they decide to go along to get along.

In the normal course of development, as teenagers move from a Level 2 to a Level 3 understanding of the world, their range of outside influences will broaden to include teachers, coaches, and pop culture—including all forms of media. Still, it will be a while before they learn that not all outside sources of advice are equally valid.

Hollywood wields enormous power to define what is acceptable and normal for the Outside-In understanding of Level 3. The popular media often present only the positive aspects of destructive behaviors, such as engaging in casual sex. Therefore it is necessary that this media-driven perspective is balanced with other sources, such as parents, mentors, youth leaders, etc. Older teens and young adults at Level 3 can make poor choices that may take years to overcome. Most young adults moving into their mid- to late-twenties start to realize some outside sources can be trusted and some cannot. Unfortunately, the school of hard knocks is often the teacher, and the beginning of Inside-Out understanding usually doesn't come without some scars to show for it. Scars, though, are a sign of healing and progress. The lessons adolescents learn in this formative period help them find a new source of identity and become the people they want to be.

While the formative influence of our parents and other key sources follow us into our Level 3 young adulthood, other sources also begin to hold sway. Once in the workplace, we are increasingly influenced by the culture of our work environment. The ideologies of political or religious affiliations will define to some degree our understanding of right and wrong. All these groups and influences will shape our understanding of ourselves, others, and our world.

All of us have been subject to peer pressure, especially during our school years. We have felt it in our workplaces as well. While peer pressure can be positive in terms of team productivity and fostering collaboration, it can also turn ugly. One of my most challenging assignments was with an executive who felt peer pressure to look the other way on a contract the agency could not fulfill. The problem was she felt she could not say no! A wealth of psychological literature is available concerning Groupthink and the Abilene Paradox[24] that helps explain the pressure to conform. The problem with leaders at lower levels is they are more susceptible to peer pressure than higher-level leaders. In this case I needed to help the executive see the possibility that her "no" could be her voice of integrity despite the value she placed on peer harmony.

Seeing the World Through the Eyes of Others

At Level 3 we are perhaps as classically outside-sourced as we will be at any time of our lives. The perspectives of people and groups we value and respect most inordinately shape our worldviews. Level 3s are usually idealistic and understand things as if they existed in a perfect state—one person can save a planet, my candidate will change the world, my fraternity is the best, etc. If we connect to a political cause, religious group, college fraternity or sorority, or similar organization, we will often be defined in an idealistic way and see the world through the lenses of those organizations' dogmas or of people who are part of those groups. The same dynamic can take place with friends, a strong family identity, a corporate culture, or a respected mentor.

Our experiences at Level 3, coupled with the influences of those we trust, lead to learned responses that allow us to understand what to do and how to react in different circumstances. A reasonably intelligent person who can recall and apply a wide variety of such learned responses is able to navigate a lot of different situations and may be perceived as an effective leader, especially by peers, even at a young age. But there are limitations at this stage of development. In a situation where your learned responses don't fit the reality of changing circumstances, you will not be able to find the solution because you can only rely on what you've learned from outside sources.

Just as outside influences affect a Level 3 understanding of the world, so do they affect the individual's well-being. As long as the circumstances we encounter align with our Level 3 understanding, there is harmony in life. When situations arise that contradict our Level 3 understanding, our world quickly falls apart, but if we realign our circumstances with our understanding, our sense of well-being can reappear as fast as it evaporated. In other words, at Level 3 we are prisoners of circumstance—we don't handle our circumstances: our circumstances handle us.

In July of 2007, former Atlanta Falcons superstar Michael Vick, once the highest paid player in the National Football League, was convicted of animal cruelty for his involvement in dog fighting. During one of the press conferences after the story broke, Vick revealed how he made sense of his circumstances. He wisely concluded, "I need to start running with a different crowd."

From a developmental perspective, he implied he had not determined who he was going to be, but instead had let those around him determine it for him. Because those influences were bad, Vick reaped the unfavorable consequences. Beyond that, the Atlanta Falcons and the entire NFL were forced to face detrimental results—damage to the reputation of the team and the league as well as countless millions of dollars in lost revenue from merchandising one of the most marketable figures in sports. Furthermore, the Atlanta franchise had been built around Vick's specific skills. Ironically, those who were influencing his understanding of right and wrong were outside the organization that depended on his performance. The NFL didn't fully recognize the importance of its role in shaping how Vick understood the world both inside and outside of work.

> Businesses benefit from understanding that the ongoing Vertical growth of their employees is just as important to the organization, if not more so, than the specific skill sets that determine their performance.

How Level 3 People See Themselves

At Level 3, the entire world is like a mirror, and we spend an inordinate amount of energy determining how people perceive us. If others see us as capable, competent, smart, athletic, charismatic, or articulate, that's how we see ourselves. Likewise, if we suspect that others see only our shortcomings, we see ourselves negatively. We notice only the things that are reflected back to us. Often others' perceptions—whether positive or negative—become a self-fulfilling prophecy.

In Greek mythology, Pygmalion was a sculptor who carved a statue of a beautiful woman he named Galatea, and then fell in love with it. Eventually Pygmalion's love for Galatea prompted the goddess Aphrodite to bring the statue to life. George Bernard Shaw wrote a play titled *Pygmalion* loosely based on this myth, which was the basis for the movie *My Fair Lady*.

The "Pygmalion effect" has been studied in educational theory. Research shows that teachers who treat their students as if they are bright have students who perform better than those whose teachers treat them as if they are slow, regardless of the students' innate capabilities. One way to understand the Level 3 lens is to see it in terms of this Pygmalion effect, where every outside influence helps shape our understanding of ourselves and our world.[25]

Bob Kegan, a colleague and noted psychologist who has been conducting research on Vertical development for almost forty years, says that at Level 3, "We don't have relationships; we are our relationships."[26]

In this stage, our relationships are the outside sources that define who we are, but they are always subject to the moods of others. If the relationships that define us are going well, we're going well. If the relationships that define us aren't going so well, we're worried and insecure . . . or maybe shattered. Everyone we value has an opinion that can make us feel like heroes or garbage. As one observant leader commented, "Parents are only as happy as their unhappiest child."

Think back to a significant relationship you may have had in your early twenties, when you were most likely fully Level 3 and even a silly argument could disrupt your entire existence until you made things right. My wife and I were newly married at that age, and anytime our relationship wasn't right, I wasn't right. I would spend all of my energy trying to figure out how to resolve the tension as quickly as possible. Looking back, I can see that my efforts were as much for my personal well-being as for our marriage. My understanding of myself was so closely tied to who we were together—and who I was in relation to her—that I had to mend the relationship just so I would be okay.

> At Level 3 we also tend to confuse our identity with our roles. While roles can help us understand who we are, they shouldn't define us. There is a subtle but important distinction between saying, "I am an accountant," as opposed to, "I am a person who practices accounting."

Just as it was appropriate to celebrate Level 2 when it was the normal time to be at that stage, we can celebrate Level 3 at the appropriate time as well. A person normally reaches Level 3 at around age twenty-two. So the fraternity president who is completely defined by the norms of his fraternity seems completely appropriate with his Outside-In understanding of himself, but a thirty-five-year-old sales manager who maintains his frat-boy understanding of the world seems incredibly immature because his development is arrested. It is understandable to see a twenty-year-old girl defined completely by her relationship with her boyfriend, but a forty-five-year-old coworker who still derives the majority of her identity from her husband is seen as inappropriately codependent.

It is completely normal and healthy to be defined by outside sources at twenty years of age. Yet as some of the things that define us at that age begin to have negative repercussions, we start to see the shortcomings of Level 3. When we decide we don't like how a group of people, a particular ideology, or a specific way of understanding is defining us, this awareness becomes the first sign of Inside-Out understanding. We are deciding for ourselves the kind of people we want to be and the kinds of influences we want to define us. Yet we remain outside-sourced for a while because we continue to understand someone else has to help us shape this different way of understanding.

In the case of arrested development where we remain at Level 3 as we enter our late thirties, early forties, or beyond, circumstances and the influence of others can have an inordinate and inappropriate impact on our well-being and understanding. For instance, Boyd and Emily are parents of two children, John and Gracie. By anyone's standards, they have been good parents, providing many opportunities for their kids and being involved in both of their numerous athletic and other extracurricular activities. John was accepted to a prestigious college last fall and Gracie is vice-president of her high school sophomore class.

Emily and Boyd were stereotypical "proud parents," but they didn't realize to what extent they were defined by the performance of their children until John did miserably on his first college midterms. Like a lot of other college freshmen, he had gotten caught up with the hustle of campus life and hadn't yet developed sufficient study habits. It certainly wasn't the world's worst tragedy, yet it crushed Emily anytime someone asked, "How's John doing in college?" and she had to stammer out a falsely optimistic response. She and Boyd started calling John every day to see if he was keeping up with his classwork. Meanwhile, they started pressuring Emily to do better in school even though she was excelling in all areas. At Level 3, Boyd and Emily had felt good about themselves as long as both their kids were doing well. But when one of them started to struggle just a little, they had no ability to detach and think to themselves, *We've trained him well. He will figure things out and be okay.*

At Level 3, the pressure Boyd and Emily feel is not so much about the objective performance of the child as it is how the child's performance reflects back on them. Outside-In thinking at that stage requires someone's affirmation, but in this case no one else was privy to the circumstances, performance, and relationships. Since effectiveness and happiness come from without—in an unhealthy way—Level 3 parents helplessly cede control of their own well-being to their children.

Similarly, managers whose development arrests at Level 3 can be completely defined by their roles. When sales are up and they are getting positive feedback from their bosses and subordinates, they feel confident about their ability as leaders. When something rocks the boat, however—a poor performance review, negative feedback from subordinates, a change in the order of things—they will question their ability and even their identity. They can't step out of their role as manager. All of their energy becomes focused on pleasing the boss, making sure the subordinates are happy, or putting things back in order.

Ideally, the disappointments of poor performance or unmet expectations should be seen as challenges that can fuel Vertical growth by helping us figure out who we want to be and what our real strengths and weaknesses are. They can prompt us to determine the story we want to tell from the inside out rather than continuing to respond only to Outside-In influences. When we move in this direction, the scales will begin to tip toward Level 4, and we will become increasingly and appropriately more satisfied, happy, and effective.

> Do you see the tough circumstances in your life as a classroom or a prison? It makes a difference . . . a big difference.

How Level 3 People See Others

Because the Level 3 understanding of ourselves is Outside-In, we are inclined to believe that everyone else understands themselves that way as well. (Presuming everyone else is where we are developmentally is a common trait across all levels before a person reaches Level 5.) Recall that Level 2 people think everyone else is operating out of their own self-interests because that is the way they themselves operate. Similarly, at Level 3 there is an innate belief that because I need to hold others up as a mirror to understand myself, so does everyone else. Therefore, at Level 3 it is normal, even if unnecessary, for us to want to take responsibility for the way others see themselves. As a result, a lot of time is spent trying to make sure that others feel good about themselves.

I occasionally teach an "Introduction to Psychology in the Workplace" class at the University of Georgia. I know when one of my lectures has hit a home run, and I am painfully aware when I've struck out. Often, after a strikeout, several students will come up to me and say, "Dr. Eigel, that was a great lecture. I really got what you were saying today." I smile and say thank you, but I recognize their empathy for me. They are thinking, *If I delivered a lecture that bad, I couldn't go on with my life.* But you have to admire their efforts to save my day, my self-esteem, and my well-being. It's the Level 3 way.

> Feeling another person's joy and sorrow (empathy) is a good starting point, but that's also where insecure people stop. They are afraid to be completely honest with others. Only someone who is both compassionate and secure has the courage to speak the truth, sometimes the hard truth, to people who need to hear it. A good example of this is the "little white lie"—an untruth told to spare someone's feelings. We justify such falsehoods by telling ourselves that if we spoke the truth the other person would fall apart, when in fact the lie is told to protect ourselves. Level 3 people believe they are saying the right thing by lying, but usually they are just protecting the relationship by not dealing with their own uncomfortable feelings.

At Level 3 we are very focused on unit or team morale and believe it defines success (even more so than achieving important objectives). If we, the team, are doing okay, then we, the team, are being effective, which proves I am a good leader. If there is tension then we must not be effective, our success will suffer, and it must be my fault.

> Level 3 people are intensely aware of how everyone around them feels, whether it's a one-on-one encounter or a report from peers or a supervisor. If my boss greets me

warmly on Monday morning and asks about my weekend when I walk into the office, my life is good. Conversely, if she walks by without saying a word, it shakes my world! All my energy will be devoted to figuring out what's wrong. I may call the boss's assistant and probe: "Is everything okay with the boss? Did she have a good weekend? Were we supposed to have a meeting? Did I miss something?" At Level 3, my well-being and understanding of myself are defined by someone else because I'm fully outside-sourced.

The Level 3 Leader

Joe is a thirty-eight-year-old manager of a 107-person distribution facility for a global retailer we will call Best Brand, the largest of its kind in the world. Joe has worked for Best Brand for seventeen years. His facility is located in a city of about 50,000 people. Joe is influential in his town and seems to be admired by everyone who works for him. I suspect that most of the people he manages and knows have the same positive impression I had of him when we spoke. Above all, he is extremely likable.

Joe's identity was his job. He was intensely loyal to Best Brand. We weren't a minute into our interview before he told me that even if he were the CEO of his company's chief competitor, he would feel like a failure. In addition, he frequently cited the comments of others to communicate how invaluable he was to his company. He took pride that others noted if any kind of problem arose, "People can go to Joe and he'll handle it." It was very important for him to believe his CEO and other bosses knew that, "Joe's location is one place we don't have to worry about because Joe is there, and nothing is going to go wrong when he's there."

There are two primary ways to be outside-sourced: through relationships and through a role. Relationally, people at Level 3 are generally defined by the perceptions others have—or seem to have—about them. Their self-esteem, then, is a direct result of others' opinions, no matter how accurate or inaccurate they may be. In Joe's interview, we see that he is a good example of this pervasive phenomenon.

When defined by their roles, Level 3 leaders' identities are largely shaped by their position and formal power in the organization. In a very real sense, the company has given them an identity, and they can't envision themselves apart from this role. They don't *have* the role of manager; they *are* that role. For them, it's almost impossible to distinguish the person from the position. This perception, however, makes them both arrogant and defensive—unattractive traits that erode respect and destroy teamwork. Companies need leaders who are authentic and secure, who are more than their positions or roles.

In Joe's interview, my focus was not on evaluating his behaviors, because most people would agree his behaviors are admirable. They were largely shaped by his Christian faith and his company's protocols—a company highly regarded as a responsible corporate citizen. He was aware that numerous outside sources had left their influence on him: "I watched how my grandfather lived, how my dad related to people where he worked, how the CEO runs the company. I saw how they were firm but honest, and how they took personal responsibility."

To understand his Level 3-ness, it's not as essential to know what Joe knows or does as it is to comprehend *how* he knows it. In his reliance on outside sources to make sense of his situations, and to know what to do, it was easy to see how novel circumstances cause confusion or uncertainty. He went into great detail in telling me how his Brittany spaniel had been attacked one day, seriously enough to require surgery. He was certain he knew which neighbor was responsible, but he had chosen not to confront the person. What he *said* was, "I let it go. I didn't want to embarrass my company or my family over something that's not worth the fight," and he added that the attack "is the neighbor's nightmare to live with." His response illustrates how he didn't have an adequate Inside-Out response to inform him how to handle this new and difficult circumstance, rather he was most concerned about how he would be perceived by others if he let his anger or emotions dictate his response (an Outside-In understanding). Reflection on who he was and what he stood for was limited to what he believed others would think about who he was and what he stood for.

We often hear Level 3 leaders justify their response to ethical dilemmas by saying things like, "If I made that decision, how could I show my face in church on Sunday?" In contrast, Level 4 leaders routinely respond with statements like, "If I chose that direction, how could I look at myself in the mirror?" Inside-Out understanding is very different from Outside-In understanding, and it's more effective as well.

Even as Joe allows his security and significance to be subject to the perceptions of others, he takes responsibility for the well-being of those around him. In this way, he is both *irresponsible* about his own identity and perceptions, and he is *overly responsible* for the identity and feelings of others. He believes his regular input is crucial for their morale. His top priority is to know the names and interests of all 107 people who report to him. Anyone is always welcome to drop in on him with a concern. In fact, he defined his regular interactions with them as "catastrophe insurance," explaining that his accessibility most likely preempted many potential problems.

It bothered him that during my interview with him, his office door was shut. It was only an hour or so, but he didn't want people to see his car parked outside and his door closed because they might worry something was wrong with him. It was his way of taking responsibility for their perceptions and feelings. He even took responsibility for my well-being by constantly affirming me throughout our interview. (He told me about a dozen times in one hour, "Now that's a great question!")

Clearly, Joe had moved beyond Stan's simplistic, either/or, me-first, Level 2 way of thinking we saw in the previous chapter. Joe is not only able to see what others need, but he also is willing to sacrifice his own agenda to help them achieve it. However, maintaining relationships is paramount to Joe. An overwhelming amount of his energy is spent managing those relationships and roles, protecting them from unpredictable crises, and constantly evaluating what he needs to do to maintain the relationship as a way to sustain a stable environment. If things are going well, Joe is doing well. If things are not going well for any reason, Joe is not well—outside sources are defining his well-being.

One of the difficult things about critiquing people whose development is arrested at Level 3 is they maintain a congenial connection to others and their circumstances, which is often quite likable and endearing. So, it is hard to criticize Joe's behaviors. The distastefulness of Stan's Level 2 egocentric understanding was apparent. Joe, however, knew his employees by name, wanted them to feel heard, walked the talk, paused before he acted, and cared about shareholder value and doing the right thing—all things most of us would endorse as effective management behaviors. Why would we ever want someone in this position to change?

The challenge at Level 3, however, is in seeing that such behaviors, as good as they might be, are not owned. They are only mimicked from outside sources valued by the Level 3 leader. It is clear much of Joe's understanding of the world is still Outside-In, which is the weakness of leading at Level 3. What would happen if the CEO gave Joe unethical advice . . . if a depressed economy created a reality that did not return shareholder value . . . if an employee that Joe really likes or respects does something inconsistent with Best Brand policy? What happens when the "right thing to do" is not covered in the management manual? Joe will be left trying to figure out such problems himself, and yet there is no true self to turn to. He will not grow as a leader until he internalizes his understanding of his behaviors, not just learns them.

Joe is beginning to determine for himself what he believes is the right thing to do and the type of person he wants to be. However, his persistence in seeking confirmation from various outside sources is clearly a Level 3 developmental position. If he were still in his early twenties it would be fairly normal, but at thirty-eight he should be farther along on his Map of Vertical development.

The challenge of coaching Level 3 leaders is their inability to take responsibility for their own mistakes, a factor that greatly undermines their ability to grow. Managers at Level 3 go to great lengths to blame others for their errors in judgment or their poor decisions. They're quick to point the finger at others and will waste considerable energy thinking through situations to make themselves "bulletproof" from criticism. As we previously mentioned, Level 3 leaders prefer for the team to vote on any significant decision. This effectively allows the leader to deny responsibility and deflect blame if the decision proves to be a mistake.

In one coaching assignment, a frustrated manager recounted his lack of sleep because he had eight direct reports and had to promote one. He wasn't firing anyone, so I wondered why his stress level was so high. He said he was worried the other seven reports would think less of him if he didn't promote them. I asked him what he planned to do. He explained he was going to promote who he thought his boss wanted him to promote. Since he was going to work with this person for the indefinite future, I probed to ask if he thought he should make the decision himself. He looked at me as if I'd lost my mind and shook his head. He wanted no part of the decision! I then asked, "What will happen if the person you promote fails to do the job?" He looked at me and wryly smiled, "It'll be my boss's fault!"

This manager's main goal—in fact, his only goal—was to protect himself from being responsible for his decision. Plausible deniability! At the same time, he was fiercely proud of his position at the company. In his mind, he couldn't let a bad decision jeopardize his status and prestige. Until he begins to take responsibility for decisions, he'll be stuck in a cycle of dodging responsibility and shifting blame to protect his cherished role in the organization. Ironically, this Level 3 protective strategy will ultimately put him most at risk in his role.

Moving On

The move to Level 4 is about owning one's own values, standards, and objectives—transitioning from an Outside-In to an Inside-Out perspective. I have worked with hundreds of leaders and witnessed their transitions to Level 4. The change of lens—the new way they begin to see the world—at that point is immediately apparent. They begin to react with confidence in their own values and decisions, no longer totally dependent on outside sources. They become more proactive in mitigating the impact of negative circumstances and relationships. They are able to make decisions that make sense of competing loyalties (i.e., performance versus relationship). Others perceive them as people who know what they stand for, and even those who have different opinions see them as more effective leaders.

But at Level 3, harmony indicates success. The leadership philosophy is, "Show consideration and respect, and they will follow you anywhere." And that approach works as long as things are running smoothly and no tough decisions need to be made. But when difficult, novel, or innovative decisions are necessary, the weaknesses of the Level 3 leader become apparent.

In a scenario similar to the one Karl just shared, one Level 3 manager put the problem succinctly. "I have a dilemma. I have three people on my team and only one of them can be promoted. I'm closer to one team member on a personal level than to another who is more qualified. I know it's not really right to promote my friend, and I suspect others will see what I'm doing. But if I promote the other person, I may lose a friend. Whatever I decide, someone will have hurt feelings and will no longer like and respect me." This manager's dilemma became a crisis because relational and performance goals were suddenly placed in conflict, and he was unable to instinctively put the good of the company above his own likability quotient.

Level 3 followers develop the philosophy of, "Don't rock the boat." I have worked with many people over the years who received objective feedback from their bosses that wasn't entirely positive, and their first instinct was to consider quitting their jobs rather than engage in potential conflict that can lead to positive change. Although most people still in the throes of Level 3 have enough maturity to realize that conflict shouldn't be avoided, they lack the ability to understand that conflict can actually be desirable in many situations because it leads to a better solution—an "iron sharpens iron" mentality. One typical Level 3 employee I interviewed told me, "I don't really avoid conflict; I just want to resolve it right away so the next time I see the other person in the hall, it's okay."

At Level 3 we tend to become enmeshed in the organizations or groups to which we belong. At work the policy manual and corporate culture are integral parts of who we are. I interviewed one Level 3 leader who managed a distribution facility and had 250 people reporting up through him (a situation and leader level very similar to Joe's). In a very predictable business, he was competent and well respected by his employees and by the organization. During the interview, I was impressed with one of his answers about how he handled conflict between employees, and I asked him how he learned to respond in that way. He had trouble answering the question, and I could see that he was becoming frustrated. Finally he said, "Look, Keith, it's in that manual over there on that shelf—okay?" He quickly cooled off, but I had what I needed: his understanding was still Outside-In.

At Level 3 we don't leave our interconnectedness at the workplace. We let our families, our faith communities, our political affiliations, and our peer groups define not only our understanding of ourselves, but also what we should do and how we should do it. We take on the perspective and ways of whatever group we may be affiliated with, and we are defined by its ideology.

I see this in faith communities and political groups all the time. They may believe strongly that compassion is an essential quality, that specific individuals or groups need to be held accountable for global warming, or that government is the root of all inefficiency. But the source of those beliefs (respectively) is what the preacher said during last week's sermon, a reputable *Time* article on global warming, and an outspoken talk-radio host. Individuals may still hold those same beliefs when they reach Level 4, but by that time they will have taken personal ownership of them.

When we closely follow the dogma of the groups that influence us, we often appear narrow-minded or simplistic in our views whenever those beliefs are challenged by a reality that does not integrate well into the dogma—not because the doctrine that defines us is necessarily faulty, but because we are simply parroting our Outside-In understanding. The beliefs are not yet truly ours. Inside-Out understanding will not come unless we continue to use these types of challenges to fuel growth to the next level of development.

It is very common in our early twenties to identify mentors, leaders, or others we want to be like. When we seek those people out, we are making an Inside-Out decision about who we want to influence us. Even so, we still recognize our need for a lot of outside instruction and training from numerous sources to help us develop into people of quality like our chosen role models. The transition from Level 3 to Level 4 begins when we start developing an Inside-Out perspective even as we continue to acknowledge the need for others to shape us from outside in. When we have accumulated enough challenges to our Level 3 understanding and taken ownership of our responses, the scale will tip and we become more Inside-Out than Outside-In.

Just because our views are being shaped by outside sources at Level 3 doesn't necessarily keep us from being confident about a particular position on an issue. The blind spot, however, is that we will confuse knowing a position with owning that position. And in order to do that, we need to stop trying to smooth over our challenges to make them go away and instead start embracing them. We will see how to do that in the next chapter as we follow the Map on to the next stop—Level 4.

Consider This . . .

1. Using five-year intervals from the time you were ten, describe or graph how your communication with your parents has fluctuated. When did you stop depending so heavily on them? Who took their place as your primary sources of information?

2. Based on your own memories and experiences, what are some examples of negative peer pressure you have faced? How well did you handle them?

   What examples can you recall of positive peer pressure? What did you learn?

3. What do you think it means that, at Level 3, "We don't *have* relationships; we *are* our relationships"?

4. What are some outside influences that previously defined (or perhaps currently define) you? (Peers? Children? Etc.)

5. Have you ever worked for someone like Joe? If so, what were his positive and negative characteristics? Did anything ever happen that was beyond his ability to handle with his Level 3, Outside-In perspective? If so, describe what happened and how it affected you and your team.

6. In your own words, explain the difference between *understanding* your beliefs and *owning* those beliefs.

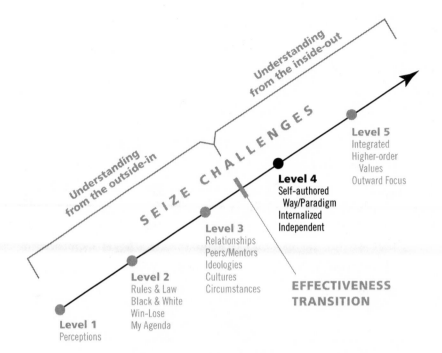

Chapter 5

LEVEL 4: TAKING OWNERSHIP OF YOUR LIFE

It would be convenient if couples or close friends could progress in their Vertical development at the same rate, but that is rarely the case. When one grows at a more rapid rate than the other(s), it turns out that both (or all) of them need to make adjustments.

Richard is a forty-five-year-old attorney at a large international law firm. He was passed over for promotion to partner almost five years ago even as several of his colleagues, including his best friend, moved up. He is married to Gwen, the beautiful mother of their two teenage boys. She was a college cheerleader and has continued her athleticism by competing in high-level tennis. Richard's career has enabled her to be a fulltime mom, and she has taken great pride in her ability to manage their home and raise their sons. Nothing is more satisfying to her than seeing her boys succeed in school and sports, both of which come easily to them.

About six months after being passed over for partner at work, Richard's father had a sudden and fatal heart attack in his late sixties. The two combined events shook Richard's world to the core. He questioned his value as a lawyer. He was unprepared to be thrust into the role of patriarch for his extended family. He was angry at the circumstances he found himself in.

But instead of chucking it all and moving to the beach, Richard went to a few of his closest friends, including Gwen, and honestly faced the fears and uncertainty those challenges had dredged up. What ensued was a new Richard who had clearer values and a stronger sense of identity. He acquired a deep understanding of the path he needed to travel to become the parent, spouse, and attorney he knew he wanted to be. In essence, those challenges, as difficult as they were, provided the impetus for Richard's understanding of himself and the world to become an Inside-Out, Level 4 individual.

Gwen noticed how engaged Richard became in his relationship to her, their children, and even his widowed mother. The leadership of his firm couldn't explain Richard's renaissance, but they saw him leading others and serving clients in a way that was truly impressive. As part of his developmental shift, Richard had taken responsibility for his reaction to his circumstances in a way that reflected a truly authentic groundedness. Shortly thereafter, Richard was invited to become a partner, and the following year he was again promoted to practice group leader—one of the top twenty positions in the firm.

Meanwhile, Gwen was not herself. She seemed short-tempered and controlling. Her oldest boy was making decisions that were, as she put it, "not who I raised him to be." She felt like she must have done something wrong. To top it off, a bit of a rift developed in her group of tennis friends over some assigned changes in partners. Gwen blamed the new captain for the anxiety the new lineup created, and for the strain placed on some of the longstanding relationships on the team. She said, "If we could just put things back the way they were, everything would be normal again."

Gwen shared her multiple frustrations with Richard, and he responded with calm assurance: "Be patient. Everything will work itself out in the long run." Much to Richard's surprise, his response only caused Gwen to be angry with him. Gwen accused him of not caring about their son and of blowing off her tennis problems as trivial.

Richard saw himself as an innocent bystander and didn't understand how she could be furious at *him*. After being unable to control or fix the circumstances that caused her frustration, Gwen's unhappiness became palpable. Richard loves Gwen, but finds his advice to "just let it go" falls on deaf ears, so he tries to keep busy with what he believes has to get done. He has effectively put Gwen in a box in his own mind, hoping things will sort themselves out soon.

In this story of Richard and Gwen, we see the challenge inherent in understanding others when they are at a different level of Vertical development. Gwen's Level 3 understanding of the world means if things aren't right, it has to be somebody else's fault, or perhaps the result of a bad situation over which she has no control. Her security and identity are continually connected to her current circumstances and the opinions of other people. And she's angry that Richard isn't as upset as he "should be" about all that's wrong in her world. She perceives his calm demeanor as a lack of compassion, and she blames him for being so uncaring. Richard doesn't understand this new tension that has developed with Gwen. He is at a loss why she wants him to be upset—he can't see how his anger or worry would help in any way.

Both of Richard's major losses—his not getting promoted and his father's death—were destabilizing. The fact that he had not made partner before his father passed away made him feel as if he had failed his dad in some way. But rather than buckling under the weight of those major challenges, he made the effort to work through them. The wisdom and strength he acquired now provides the fuel for him to become the man (husband, father, lawyer) he wants to be. In other words, by leaning into the challenges instead of attempting to avoid or downplay them, Richard made the transition to Level 4.

Richard is seeing the world through a new, improved lens. He is learning a lot as he makes progress in his Vertical development. But one thing he still needs to learn is that other people do not necessarily perceive the world the same way he does. We have made this observation before, and it's just as relevant at Level 4.

The good news is that Richard doesn't have to reverse his Vertical development to keep the peace, yet he needs to realize it's solely up to him to see things from Gwen's perspective. She can't yet understand his newfound calm or make sense of the world through a Level 4 lens, but Richard can meet her where she is because he has been there.

Those at a higher level of Vertical development must take responsibility for seeing the perspectives of those at lower levels. This is especially true at Level 4 after we make the major shift from an Outside-In to an Inside-Out perspective. Gwen is still looking for outside affirmation for her beliefs, and telling her to "just let it go" sounds like insanity to someone trying to cope at Level 3. Richard will soon learn that when he meets others where they are, he will become more effective at facilitating their growth. That is what great leaders, including parents and spouses, do.

> The transition from Level 3 to 4 focuses on taking responsibility in every part of your life. For example, there may be a person in your organization right now whom you would rather not have to deal with. The Level 3 leader minimizes time with such people—avoiding or ignoring them—because interacting with them is so difficult. The Level 4 leader, on the other hand, takes responsibility for the relationship and finds a way to make it more productive. Challenges, even in broken relationships, force us to reevaluate and grow, so the areas where we are most significantly challenged (for many of us, our careers) are where we grow first into Level 4. However, becoming fully Level 4 means we need to be challenged in all the other areas of our lives. If the challenges don't come on their own, we can intentionally identify and lean into opportunities in those areas.

Seeing the World from the Inside Out

If we, like Richard, learn to seize challenges for growth, we will begin to *self-author* areas of our understanding, meaning that the way we see the world, ourselves, and others will depend less on the influence of outside sources. This shift often begins by the time we reach our early- to mid-thirties.

As Karl noted, we first develop an Inside-Out perspective in the areas where we have the most experience or spend most of our time because that's where we have the greatest probability of encountering challenges that will contradict our current lens. Challenging circumstances are the catalysts that provide the potential for growth to the next level. If your primary leadership role is in the home, that's almost certainly the first place you will stop being dependent on outside sources, and it's there that you will likely begin to open your understanding of yourself in relationship to others and to the demands of running a household. Likewise, if your primary leadership role is at work, you may begin to own what you believe to be true in that environment sooner than you will in others. And if you acquire expertise in a particular subject, you likely will begin to self-author in that area before you will in other areas.

Similarly, if you are an active part of your faith community or a political organization, you will certainly encounter contradictions to your beliefs, and those contradictions will leave you two options: keep letting other outside sources determine what you believe, or do the difficult work of reconciling the contradictions from the inside out. The former can arrest your development; the latter will lead to growth.

As you move closer to Level 4 and farther away from Level 3, you will become increasingly irritated by those outside sources that demand to have influence over you. Even as you get to the "Entering Level 4" road sign on the Map, you may find yourself getting angry because circumstances or relationships are still trying to define you. By that point, however, you should realize *you* are the one who decides whether you get angry or not. This awareness is another proof of Vertical growth. There's a difference between saying "He made me angry," and "I got angry when he did that." When *he* makes you angry, you're being "done to" from the outside in. But when *you* get angry that someone did something, you're taking responsibility for the anger from the inside out.

When we are "done to," we are left with several bad options: blaming the offender, excusing ("He couldn't help it"), minimizing the hurt ("It wasn't that bad"), running away, or trying to act as if nothing happened. When we take responsibility, we recognize we are accountable for our response. We may feel hurt or anger (or both), but we wade into our emotions and find the right path for the situation. At Level 4 we take responsibility for ourselves because we gain an Inside-Out understanding of everything (world, self, and others). Reflecting on how to take responsibility for your most visceral emotions can actually be a great tool for intentionally accelerating your own growth.

> Albert Einstein observed, "How many people are trapped in their everyday habits; part numb, part frightened, part indifferent? To have a better life we must keep choosing how we're living."
>
> You create your own path by being genuine, being yourself, and exercising your personal freedom. For the first time, a Level 4 leader can make personal value decisions that are in the best interest of the institution—without arrogance or timidity. Such leaders can take a stand *from* their values.

Today, most of us work in complex work environments that are physically and emotionally demanding. Dealing with conflict is a way of life. How well do you handle conflict? Your identification of the source of the conflict says a lot about your stage of development. For example, how many times have you said, "My boss upsets me"? Of course, the problem with that statement is that you are letting another person decide whether or not you are upset. You are defined and shaped by the other person's opinion of you, which indicates more Level 3 thinking. At Level 4, people see through a different lens, and they realize they have far more choices than ever before. They can choose to not let others determine their emotions. Instead, they can say to themselves, "I get upset when my boss says or does that." They choose their response, even their emotions. At Level 4, the person isn't an emotional puppet on the boss's string of praise or blame. The boss's opinion matters for people in Level 4, of course, but it doesn't define them.

As a population statistic, becoming fully Level 4 typically takes place around our mid-forties, which is when we see one of two outcomes. Those who confront the challenges and do the difficult work of transitioning from Outside-In to Inside-Out thinking undergo a midlife *transition*—a time when we determine who we are going to be, what we are going to believe, and what contribution we want to make. It is no coincidence that this is the period of life when those in the working world will hit their "power years" in terms of productivity, influence, and earning potential. When you know who you are and what you stand for, and when you have an Inside-Out understanding of how the world works, people are much more likely to follow you. Your effectiveness as a leader dramatically increases because of your Level 4 way of making sense of things.

The other outcome, for those who remain entrenched at Level 3 and refuse to move on, is not a midlife transition but a midlife *crisis*. Hollywood, of course, has presented a familiar stereotype of the midlife crisis, especially in men. The scenario goes something like this: A family man begins to feel disconnected from his world, disturbed by his physical decline, disappointed with how his kids are turning out and the distance he feels from his wife, and frustrated that his life seems to have no purpose. His response—in the movies, at least—is to trade in the minivan for a red sports car, quit his job and his family, and start dating women only slightly older than his daughter. We see this scenario as simultaneously funny and sad because we likely know people who have done similar things. In terms of Vertical development, these characters simply traded one set of outside influences for another, rather than responding to an opportunity to grow. Sadly, in such real-life scenarios it is often the second or even third wife who reaps the benefit of the positive development that could (and should) have taken place when the crisis first arose.

Life is series of frequent changes that range from welcomed to catastrophic. We escape a bad boss by leaving the company and finding a better work environment, but we lose our house in a fire. There's big difference between *change* and *transition*: change is situational, and transition is psychological. Change refers to outside events or conditions that happen to us. Transition is how we learn and grow so we can make sense of the event. As a general in the United States Army said to me in an interview, "It's not what happens *to* you that matters, but what happens *in* you." Being fired may not be the end of the world. We may find great relief in getting fired because we're escaping a Level 2 boss! It's not the news; it's what you do with that news.

Transitions—moving from one level to the next—create challenges and contradictions that reveal what's important to us. They provide the opportunity to understand others and ourselves in a different, transformational way. However, transitions don't come easily or smoothly. Many (if not most) of the significant events that lead to transitions from one Vertical level to the next come from disruptive and disorienting life events. But even in the worst events in our lives, we can find the seeds of new growth.

Even under the healthiest of circumstances, making the transition from Level 3 to Level 4 is never easy. It is difficult not to blame others or hold our circumstances responsible for continuing to define who we should be. But if we plow through and self-author our own understanding, the reward is great. At Level 4, for the first time, we discover a self who can authentically lead. The transition marks the beginning of truly effective leadership. It's not where you're leading *to* that matters; it's where you're leading *from*.

Up until Level 4, the source of our understanding—how we know what we know or what we believe to be true about how the world works and what is important in life—comes from outside sources. As Level 3 twenty-somethings, those beliefs are largely shaped by friends, family, and affiliations. Eventually, however, challenging experiences will necessarily call many such beliefs into question. Becoming Level 4 requires at least a temporary letting go of those outside-sourced beliefs in order to enable our crucial perceptions to start forming from within. As we have said, the *content* of what we know doesn't necessarily change, but our *ownership* of it does.

For many people the most poignant example of this transition has to do with faith—specifically, what they hold to be true about God. Whether raised in a religious or non-religious home, most feel a tremendous pull to be at least partially defined by the spiritual beliefs of our families. (This is true whether we try to emulate the beliefs of our parents or if we don't like what we see and determine to go some opposite direction.) The influences of those beliefs—often deep-seated from childhood—can define us for much of our early adulthood.

Doubt and questions will inevitably arise, becoming the challenges that contradict our current understanding. If we suppress or ignore those challenges, development is arrested and others will perceive our beliefs as shallow and indefensible, not something they would necessarily want to emulate. However, if we persist through the difficult work of struggling with the doubts and questions that contradict our current understanding, we eventually gain confidence in *why* we believe what we believe, and others will see in us a depth that is much more compelling.

Although this Inside-Out understanding is often easier to illustrate in matters of belief or other ideologies like political affiliation, the concept applies to all that we hold to be true about how the world works. The ability to demonstrate an Inside-Out take on the world is the mark of an effective leader that evokes followership, whether in ideological matters, the business world, or family life.

At Level 4 you don't want someone else to lay out every step that needs to be taken, and you don't look to outside sources to figure out what to believe and how to respond to any given situation. What you desire is a self-defined goal because you know what to do and what success means. However, this self-authored understanding of your performance does not guarantee that you will be effective or that your goals are necessarily good ones. There is an amorality to Level 4 that does not presuppose "rightness." The common thread at Level 4 isn't the beliefs or values we hold; it's that those things are self-determined—they are held from the inside out.

Success at Level 4 can create a subtle danger. The more success we achieve in using our new paradigm, the more certain we are of its effectiveness. But as we employ this new paradigm that works so well, are we leading out of rigidity or confidence? It's a fine line. We can lead effectively from either side of that line for a while, but rigidity will ultimately lead to irrelevance as the world continues to change. Even though our effectiveness at Level 4 is far beyond what it has ever been, we need to keep our eyes on the Map and see that we still have room to grow, and that growth won't take place without a willingness to keep changing.

Winston Churchill remarked, "The price of greatness is responsibility." The hallmark of Level 4 leaders is their ability to craft their own way of making decisions. Their "own way" originates out of strongly held values and principles honed over years of experience, not out of a desperate need to be right like people at Level 2. Also, Level 4 people lead with confidence more than out of arrogance. But beware: Level 4 security and confidence can be mistaken for cockiness by those who haven't yet experienced the strength of this Inside-Out level of development.

Level 4 leaders are so often successful at leading others because they are secure enough to listen and confident enough to make hard decisions, which, in turn, engenders confidence in their leadership. Level 4 leaders are defined by their values. Leaders at all levels can have strong values, but Level 4 leaders have integrated them into their identity, demeanor, and communication. Understandably, it takes time and experience to reach this stage of personal development. We seldom meet Level 4 leaders under the age of thirty-five.

We said earlier that we speak of Level 3 leaders as being their relationships or roles more than having them. Similarly, at Level 4, more than merely having our values, we *are* those values.

How Level 4 People See Themselves

Another part of self-authoring one's own understanding involves knowing oneself. At Level 4 we no longer look to others as a mirror to reflect our self-understanding the way we did at Level 3. We now have a satisfying ownership and understanding of our strengths, weaknesses, and contributions. We create for ourselves the standards we want to live up to, so we don't need someone else to tell us that we've done a good or a bad job. The mirror you use at Level 4 is the one in which you see your own reflection as both chief critic and chief supporter.

Of course, you still have the opportunity to seek out feedback from others, and most effective leaders do. It will aid in your continued growth, but it is no longer merely a measure of how you're doing as it was at Level 3. No longer will the feedback from others *define* you, rather it *refines* you. At Level 4 you have a confidence that comes from knowing who you are, and then you can seize feedback as a challenge to your understanding that will provide fuel for continued growth. Those who always reject the feedback of others, especially when it contradicts their understanding, begin to appear rigid or closed, and their effectiveness will never realize its potential.

Finally, at Level 4 you no longer hold others responsible for how you feel. Earlier, we highlighted the difference between saying "You made me angry," and "I felt angry when you did that." The first statement assigns blame; the second assumes responsibility. In all emotions, not just anger, you tend to be more stable and satisfied at Level 4 because you stop blaming others or circumstances when things go wrong. When you take responsibility for your emotions, you can be the author of your well-being even in the midst of challenging situations.

Eleanor Roosevelt was accurate when she said, "No one can make you feel ashamed without your permission." That is, no one can make you feel anything that you don't want to feel, including anger, sadness, or guilt. It's your choice . . . at least, it's a choice for those at Level 4.

How Level 4 People See Others

When we become able to understand ourselves with Inside-Out independence at Level 4, we also begin to grant others the autonomy and freedom to do things differently than we do, even when we don't agree with how they're doing it. However, as we saw from the example of Richard and Gwen, people at Level 3 (or below) might not be ready for this degree of autonomy. They still need help in understanding their world, themselves, and how they should interact with others. Therefore, Level 3 followers can misinterpret the Level 4 leadership style as detached, uncaring, or aloof, even though the intention is to give them more freedom to be themselves.

Since you don't expect others to be responsible for your self-esteem at Level 4, the idea that you might be responsible for someone else's self-esteem seldom crosses your mind. People who report to Level 4 leaders frequently complain that they don't receive positive feedback, only criticism. Level 4 leaders need to recognize that those who look to them for leadership may be so tied to (and defined by) the goal or initiative that they might take any sort of criticism (even about the goal or initiative) personally. While the freedom that comes from not being shaped or defined by the opinion of others can greatly increase your Level 4 effectiveness, you can find yourself facing unintended negative consequences if you don't realize the impact you can have on people who are developmentally where you once were.

In the context of home life, well-intentioned Level 4 people who grant other family members autonomy can be perceived as detached or uncaring (as Richard learned with his "Get over it" advice). It is incumbent upon Level 4s to adjust to the level of their partners, because asking the other person to make sense of the world and the relationship from a Level 4 perspective is something he or she is not yet able to do.

> Great leaders don't insist that others meet them at their level; they are adept at going to where the others are.

Effectiveness at Level 4

It is not until we reach Level 4 that we have the opportunity to become truly effective.

> We say "opportunity" because it is completely possible (though not at all likely) to self-author an ineffective understanding or paradigm. Plenty of people have endured heartaches and learned lessons, but occasionally the lessons they learn reinforce their fears, self-pity, and defensiveness instead of leading them to open new doors to wisdom, security, and hope. The difficulties we face show us the doors to the next level of development, but not everyone walks through them. Some turn and walk away. People who arrive at Level 4 have walked through those doors, often many of them.

Prior to becoming Level 4, what passes for effectiveness are the knowledge, skills, and abilities we bring to the table—our Lateral development. Twenty-somethings who demonstrate a higher level of intelligence, communication ability, expertise, and/or charisma than their more "average" peers are perceived as potential leaders.

Yet in most cases a charismatic, Level 3, twenty-seven-year-old is not viewed as effective a leader as a grounded, Level 4, fifty-year-old with less charisma. And if the knowledge, skills, and abilities are essentially equal, the difference in effectiveness between a Level 3 and Level 4 leader becomes even more apparent.

At a two-day talent evaluation meeting with a Fortune 100 subsidiary, I heard the word *gravitas* used repeatedly to describe the next-generation leaders whom the executive team believed to have the highest potential. The Latin root for *gravitas* means "seriousness," but the way they used it suggested an independent and confident *groundedness* desirable in those being considered for the highest levels of leadership. They were looking for leaders who knew who they were and what they stood for, and who had the ability to communicate those things—in other words, Level 4 leaders.

It only makes sense that you will be more effective at understanding yourself, others, and the world at each successive level, because you retain and better understand the perspective you had at each previous level. The reason there is such a jump at Level 4 is because this is the first stage where you can take ownership and responsibility for the use of the influences and factors that defined you at the previous levels.

To illustrate this, here are two normal distributions that come from research I did on the relationship between Vertical development and leader effectiveness. The distribution on the top shows the level scores of more than one thousand highly educated professionals.[27] As we would expect, these scores confirm that the ability to grow Vertically is distributed normally throughout the population because they roughly fit the bell curve.

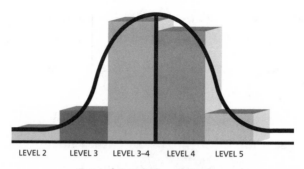

LEVEL 2   LEVEL 3   LEVEL 3–4   LEVEL 4   LEVEL 5

General Population of Leaders
The Distribution of Leader Level Scores for the General Population of Leaders.

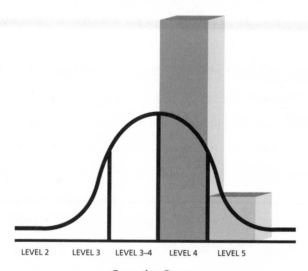

LEVEL 2   LEVEL 3   LEVEL 3–4   LEVEL 4   LEVEL 5

Executive Group
The Distribution of Leader Level Scores for the Executive Group.

The second distribution reflects the Vertical development of chief executives from twenty Fortune 500, industry-leading, public companies. This group of leaders had been elected by their companies' boards of directors who had a fiduciary interest at stake in choosing the right leader. Leader effectiveness is a hard thing to measure holistically, but by controlling for tenure and performance in the industry, I attempted to confirm each board's assessment that the chosen leaders were as effective as they believed. The Vertical development of this second group was Level 4 and up. If Vertical development had no relationship to effectiveness, we would have expected the scores of this group to be distributed similar to the previous population.

> This research supports the anecdotal evidence that many researchers over the past decades have purported to be true: first, the higher your level, the more effective you are as a leader; and second, you don't truly become an effective leader until you reach a place of self-authorship at Level 4.

The Level 4 Leader

Kate is a prime example of a Level 4 leader. She is fifty-four years old, married, and has two kids in their early twenties. She works on her regional CEO's executive team for (at the time of our interview) one of the three largest banks in the United States. In addition to her fulltime job, she volunteers in the community as a member of the school board in her county.

Kate made a decision about midway through her career that she did not want to be a top executive, but preferred to serve under that person. With all the power plays in the corporate world, she took intentional steps to let others know that power grabbing was not her intent. Ironically, her decision actually increased her influence as a leader—especially with those above her, but also with her peers and those who report to her.

Her comments reflect great self-awareness, often characteristic of Level 4 leaders, and in addition to strengths and weaknesses, her awareness also includes values, standards, and motivation. She says, "Nothing would make me happier than for it to say on my tombstone that she was a person of integrity and compassion."

Kate highly values relationships and being influential in the development of others. She told me at numerous points, "I do my homework," which included knowing the strengths of those she works with, enabling her to build a strong team and guide them to mutually satisfying decisions. But like most all Level 4 leaders, she is not enmeshed in those relationships. When she needs to, she can dismiss a team member who consistently refuses to pull his or her weight. She can set aside relationships and how others feel about her for the good of the company, something a Level 3 manager can rarely do. Yet even those decisions are rooted in compassion. While reflecting over having to fire a programmer four months previously, she told me, "He wasn't on the same page with the rest of us. We gave him some boundaries that he didn't respect and he painted himself into a corner that he couldn't get out of. My prayer for that guy is that after he gets over his hurt and has moved on he will actually acknowledge that this was the right decision."

Kate's value system influences how she leads people. She commented, "I think a desire to be compassionate toward people is probably the basis of how I begin to make a decision, but being compassionate doesn't imply being weak. I believe a lot in tough love. I look at the seed of the problem and then, depending on the environment I'm in—professional, personal, or community—I have to do what is best in that case. For instance, my utmost responsibility for the business is to avoid putting the business at risk." Such an Inside-Out perspective allows her to be compassionate and still let people go who repeatedly fall short of the standards that will lead to the success of the organization.

Early in the interview Kate observed that, "parenting and managing are very similar." She went on to explain that she had realized that one of the most important things she could do for her two teenagers was prepare them to be independent and confident enough to face both the good and difficult issues of life on their own. She carried the same philosophy into her management style for her employees.

She also modeled that philosophy in her own work life. She described a challenging assignment she was just completing. The Vice President of Information Technology had resigned over a year previously. The division President attempted to take on his responsibilities for a couple of months, but it was more than he could handle with his other duties. He told Kate, "You're going to have to go over there and run that department, and figure out what's going on," even though Kate confessed that she hardly knew enough about IT to turn on her own computer.

It turned out that the previous manager had not done a good job at all. The place was a mess. But Kate carefully studied the situation. Later, she reflected, "Everything was wrong. But in twelve months we stabilized the department. We stabilized the system. We hired a manager. We restructured the departments. I got approval to hire twenty-one new people. And today things are stable because of what we worked through. For me, that's success." It certainly is. It is also a demonstration of how a Level 4 leader can function even in an area completely outside her field of expertise.

What's important to see in Kate is how she is being *for* people in her organization and not just being *beside* them or even being *with* her subordinates and peers. Being *for* them means she is invested in others' development and growth. How many leaders delegate just to offload work they don't want to do, concerned more about what they need than what the organization needs? But a Level 4 leader delegates to enable team members to develop skills, gain experience, and perform more effectively—not just in their current position, but also in preparation for their next one. Being *for* your subordinates emerges out of a genuine concern for them and for what the organization needs to achieve.

Throughout the interview I wondered how Kate had gotten to this stage of development, and toward the end it came out. In response to a question about her value system, she said, "My intense value system probably developed to the strength that it is now just over the last five years. My husband was unemployed for fourteen months after a company downsizing, and it was tough. At the same time I had to assume the responsibility of care for my dad. He was diagnosed with Alzheimer's, and several other things were wrong. Three years ago I lost my grandmother, who was my model of unconditional love. So all of those experiences have culminated in my understanding that what was really important was the compassion that people showed me."

This interview took place several years ago, and Kate's boss is one of the CEOs who took part in my research. He has kept up with Kate, and he says that she is greatly admired for her leadership ability and effectiveness. In his own way, he describes her as Level 4 leader. "She knows who she is and what she is about," he said.

Think about how pleasant and productive it would be to work for someone like Kate—a leader who knows who she is and what she should do from the inside out. She is a prime example of a Level 4 leader who might soon become one of the fifteen percent of people who continue growing to Level 5. She already engages in things like serving the growth needs of others by meeting them where they are, maintaining humility about her own contributions, being open to understanding the perspectives of others, and intentionally evaluating her experiences to see where she may need to loosen her grip—all Level 5 behaviors, although she is still seeing through a Level 4 lens.

Those hovering at Level 4 have three options. The first is painful, and we have no control over it. Some of us will experience (not by choice) circumstances that create new challenges and contradictions: the death of a loved one, the loss of a job, financial hardship, a divorce, an illness, or some other calamity. Eventually, life may deal a difficult hand that will force us to reevaluate our Level 4 lens. When this happens, we usually are unprepared and growth is very difficult.

A second option to get unstuck at Level 4 is to intentionally serve others in ways that lead to their development. This will cause our Level 4 understanding to be challenged and contradicted, because as we authentically seek to understand the ways others see and do things, we will begin to see that ours is not the only valid way.

> The third option is to stay where we are, arrested at this stage of development because it's perceived safer and involves less risk. Of course, by not taking the risk to grow, you put your career, company, yourself, and even your family at greater risk. Unfortunately, this is what most people do. That's why at this stage, more than ever, we need to consult our Map and make our way on toward our final destination.

Moving On

The vast majority of people who make it to Level 4 arrest their development there. Research suggests that up to eighty-five-percent of the population stops growing at Level 4 or below. Why? One big reason is the older we get, the more resources we have to protect ourselves from the kinds of challenges and contradictions that can lead to development. When hardships arise—especially for people who have learned to self-author a way that has led to great success—it's not difficult to insulate oneself from those unpleasant circumstances. Vacations, afternoons at the club, golf, or a bottle of good wine can take our minds off of late-in-life challenges that could help us continue to grow. Other distractions are available for those who aren't as wealthy: television, beer, or simply hanging around with like-minded friends can serve the same purpose.

Without continued challenge and contradiction, which are essential to growth, a Level 4 lens will become increasingly fixed, especially if great success allows new challenges to be easily avoided or purchased away. Why should I change my way of doing things if it's working?

The self-authorship of Level 4, which makes such a positive difference in leadership, was created (authored) in an environment that is not stagnant. It is changing, and therefore our understanding must also change to stay relevant in the current environment. Relevance is what Level 5 leaders develop: they stay grounded in the things that don't change—the values that underpin the generational differences—but remain open to new ways of realizing those values.

Consider This . . .

1. Do you know a couple like Richard and Gwen who underwent some relational conflicts because they were at different stages of developmental growth? If so, how were those difficulties resolved?

2. Have you made the transition from Outside-In to Inside-Out thinking? How can you tell? If you've made this transition, in what *specific* area of your life did that shift begin? Explain. How has that change made a difference in the way you see yourself, the world, and others?

3. What experience, if any, have you had with either a midlife transition or a midlife crisis?

4. What's the difference between letting input from others *define* you and letting it *refine* you?

5. Have you ever worked for or with a leader like Kate? If so, what did you learn from the experience?

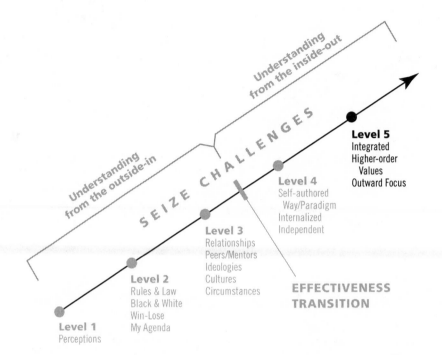

Chapter 6

LEVEL 5: LETTING GO AND RISING ABOVE

Years ago I visited my grandparents almost every Friday for lunch. They lived on the eleventh floor of a high-rise retirement community serviced by the slowest elevator in the history of commercial construction. Some days they fully intended to meet me at noon but didn't make it to the ground floor until twenty past. (I'm not exaggerating.) On those days, I had plenty of time to visit with some of the residents in the lobby. I frequently got into conversations with sweet-looking, blue-haired people, many of whom had little good to say about my generation. Their anger, frustration, and discontent were palpable because they believed we were leading the world to hell in a handbasket. My way was not their way, and they made sure I knew it. This experience is a great image of what it is like to interact with someone whose development has been arrested at Level 4 for way too long.

On other days, though, I would talk with sweet-looking, blue-haired people who seemed to hold in their hands the wisdom of the ages, and I would secretly hope that my grandparents would be running even later than usual. Those people could see the things our generations had in common and share penetrating insights about my circumstances, even though my generation was forty or fifty years removed from theirs. I also noticed they had a peace about them, a contentment about their circumstances that came from having a broader perspective on life. I later understood this as being Level 5.

Seeing the World More Clearly Than Ever

In the previous chapter, we stated that as few as fifteen percent of people—possibly fewer—keep growing beyond Level 4. But that statistic does not mean reaching Level 5 is reserved for a fortunate few who are exceptional in some way. Almost everyone willing to keep growing can reach Level 5, and this progress doesn't depend on education or intelligence.

One of my favorite Level 5 people was a seventy-five-year-old brick mason with a sixth-grade education. He was an African-American who grew up during the Depression and had worked the first half of his adult life under segregation. He missed out on many of the opportunities most people presume will facilitate Vertical growth, and yet he possessed an enviable wisdom. He was a respected leader in his circles of influence as well as with the crew who worked for him. He was completely content with who he was and an inspiration to everyone he met.

What is it that makes Level 5 leaders so effective? As we have learned, at each level of development all of our previous lenses are at our disposal. Even after we move to a more effective way of seeing, we can utilize and take a perspective on all our previous levels of understanding. This additive nature of the Vertical journey explains why our understanding becomes more comprehensive and accurate as we continue to grow, as well as why Level 5 leaders exhibit such great wisdom.

From our coaching work we know Level 5 leaders make better decisions. This should not be a surprise because Level 5 leaders do not make decisions based on their own self-interests. One Level 2 coaching client said he walks into every room and looks around to see if he is the smartest person there. What are the chances this guy is going to make team-based decisions that are in the best interest of the institution? Level 5 leaders do not go along to get along. Their impulse is not to take a vote so they can avoid personal responsibility for any potential failures. Rather, they make sure everyone is heard and that the team walks out of the meeting not necessarily in total agreement, yet committed to the decision. Level 5 leaders are more open to hearing what is new in the situation than Level 4 leaders, and they try to expand the vision of the entire team.

At Level 5 we are able to take an objective view of even ourselves. The hard-won Level 4 understanding—the self-authored paradigm we (in most cases) spend forty-plus years creating—yields a clearer, Inside-Out understanding of self, others, and the world.

Yet technically this new and broader perspective isn't one we have, rather, it still has us. In the move to Level 5, our self-authored, Level 4 perspective increasingly becomes something we can step away from. It no longer defines us. The new lens we discover at Level 5 provides the ability for the first time to combine different paradigms into a larger whole. Although not quite as obvious as some of the previous lenses, this larger whole is the filtering mechanism through which we make sense of all those previous lenses.

The less-tangible lens through which we understand ourselves, others, and the world is best understood as a system of principles and values. This Level 5 perspective includes openness, honesty, courage, justice, selflessness, productivity, service, respect for the inherent value of others, authenticity, and vulnerability.

Clear, compelling values are critical for effective leadership. At Level 5 we become stronger in our convictions, primarily because we understand ourselves and we know we can't effectively lead others without those convictions. Values and convictions drive effective behavior. You have probably seen plenty of decisions made because of the "political winds" in a company, a family, or any other group of people, instead of from self-authored convictions.

From our research, we can detect little, if any, deviation among Level 5 values across gender, nationality, or culture. They are universally recognized as good and right. Psychologist Robert Kegan called them a universal set of higher-order values.[28] C.S. Lewis and others have referred to them as the Tao.[29] However, simply agreeing that these principles are true and right does not mean you are at Level 5. The key to reaching Level 5 is the willingness to let go of not only your paradigm, but even the values you authored at Level 4. It is a destabilizing process, yet one that allows the new organizing principles to emerge.

> It seems incomprehensible to people at Levels 2 or 3, but Level 5 leaders are effective precisely because they live in the tension of the contradiction of their opposing values. For instance, consider the competing values of maintaining a loving, supportive family and achieving excellence at work. In today's workplace these are seen as distinct choices: "Do I leave work early to see my daughter's volleyball match, or do I stay and get the project done?" Level 5 leaders effectively deal with the contradictions by resisting either/or closure. They know opposites exist and feel comfortable with them. They consider the options and make the best decision for the moment, although they may make a different decision next time. They hold both values in their hands, honoring both and neglecting neither.

From a Level 5 perspective, your new and final lens will make sense of the world, others, and even yourself, allowing you to more easily "rise above it all." In the transition out of Level 4, you will increasingly incorporate higher-order values into who you are, and the emerging Level 5 lens will increasingly filter or make sense of everything around you—including your identity, goals, relationships, choices, and legacy—through these values.

Why were the people in my grandparents' retirement community who were at Level 5 the rare exception to the more typical, cranky old people? Most of the residents had adhered to their paradigm far beyond its relevance, which provided an eye-opening preview of where we are headed if we allow success at Level 4 to arrest our growth. For some people, it might take a catastrophic challenge (like losing a child or suffering grave illness) to shatter the developmental concrete that has set around them before they turn their energy to understanding and serving the growth needs of others. Others, however, will simply choose to be less critical of younger people who frustrate them and more interested in the perspective and developmental opportunities of that younger generation. When they do, they will begin knitting a new understanding that can bring the generational differences into a common whole.

When the self-authored paradigms we held at Level 4 no longer define our understanding, we can take an increasingly objective view of ourselves and compare our paradigms to those of others. This ability to rise above ourselves is what we perceive as wisdom in Level 5 leaders, and it explains why we feel understood, enlightened, and energized when we are around such highly developed individuals.

It's good for society when parents attempt to raise principled, respectful children instilled with Level 5 values. However, a principled and ethical twenty-five-year-old is certainly not Level 5. It is not behavior that determines level of development, but rather the lens through which those behaviors that define—as well as limit— understanding are understood. That said, even from Level 3, it is to our benefit to engage in the behaviors and adopt the values of Level 5 leaders through our Level 3, Outside-In lens. Doing so will propel development as we continue to take advantage of the challenges that can accelerate growth toward a Level 5 destination.

When our behaviors and values are consistent with Level 5 behaviors and values, then eventual growth to Level 5 will only require changing the lens through which we see the world, ourselves, and others, not the values and behaviors as well. When Level 4 leaders self-author an understanding that is not as open or service-minded, the transition to Level 5 is more difficult, because in addition to the difficult work of changing their lens, they have to create a new set of behaviors and priorities as well. We all have known Level 4 leaders whose values are characterized more by achievement of objectives than by selflessness, by self-protection more than vulnerability, by promoting their own way more than serving others, and by maintaining their system more than being authentic. Regardless of one's level, it facilitates growth to ask, "What is the most generous, most helpful, or most service-minded thing I can do?" Not only does this orientation benefit others, but ironically it also promotes personal growth.

When the higher-order ethic of Level 5 becomes our lens, it also becomes the organizing principle by which we view all of our previous lenses. This means that the rules, order, and self-interest of Level 2, the outside influences of Level 3, and the effectiveness of our self-authored Level 4 paradigm are all understood through the Level 5 lens of justice, mercy, goodwill, honesty, courage, and valuing others. Level 5 understanding, even as it comes from within, will be directed outward for the benefit of others. One hundred percent of the Level 5 leaders we have interviewed confirm with their behaviors that this serving-the-growth-of-others orientation may be the best way to move from Level 4 to Level 5. In the context of truly understanding and serving the growth needs of others, we are able to gain an increasingly more accurate view of ourselves.

As we have said (and will consider further), the focus on others rather than themselves is evident in many of our national and world heroes. Yet most of us know other Level 5 leaders who are incredibly wise, usually advanced in years, and not at all famous—perhaps aunts or uncles, grandparents, neighbors, bosses, clients, professors, or pastors. We recognize their wisdom because they rise above the tension that tends to separate generations. They see the principles and values behind the challenges everyone faces. It is this ability to perceive what we have in common through the lens of higher-order values and principles that allows Level 5 leaders to connect across generations, ideologies, and cultures. They continue to grow as individuals even as they promote the development of others to the highest levels. This way of making sense of the world gives the Level 5 leader the capacity to integrate complex and seemingly opposing perspectives into a cohesive whole.

This is a topic for another entire book, but I believe that when we look at the life of Jesus through this Level 5 prism, the apparent paradoxes in some of his behaviors are resolved. Some people are bothered by differences (i.e., the paradoxical values of justice vs. mercy, or truth vs. love) that, seen through earlier lenses, often seem like contradictions. But using a Level 5 lens, those teachings become remarkably consistent and easily reconciled in light of a higher-order perspective.

Even though we become open to evaluating different "ways" or paradigms at Level 5, that doesn't mean we won't have a preferred way of doing things. Rather, our preferred way will not limit our capacity to realize the higher-order values that are now the lens through which we see and understand our worlds. We become able to take an objective view of our preferred paradigm, which was something we couldn't do at Level 4. Even though we may prefer this paradigm as a way of understanding the world, from Level 5 we become able to step back, evaluate it through our Level 5 lens, and incorporate it into these higher-order values.

> Oddly enough, one of the biggest impediments to moving to Level 5 is success. When your Level 4 way of seeing the world has been successful, you are inclined to see it as the best (and perhaps only) way. The longer you maintain your Level 4 way of understanding, the harder the developmental concrete sets around you. As we said earlier, the problem with not changing is that as the world keeps changing around you, your paradigm will eventually lose its relevance as a way to effectively deal with others, the world, and even yourself.

How Level 5 Leaders See Themselves

At Level 5, we are by definition more self-aware than at any previous level. In taking this increasingly objective view of ourselves (which only happens at Level 5), we become more insightful into our strengths and weaknesses. Because we are others-oriented and open to contrasting views, we will naturally continue to reevaluate and refine our understanding of ourselves—this refinement is the process of becoming increasingly Level 5.

This capacity to view ourselves objectively also promotes humility. We often appear egocentric at Level 4 because we believe our new Inside-Out perception of the world is the best way, otherwise we wouldn't have self-authored it in the first place. Yet at Level 5 our objectivity increases. We view ourselves in the context of the larger world, recognizing that our way isn't the only way. When we realize others potentially have just as good (if not better) visions, values, and ways, humility is a natural byproduct.

Level 5 leaders have a different level of self-awareness than those at any of the previous levels of development. They have the remarkable ability to hold their Level 4 identity and values at arm's length and take an objective view of their strengths and weaknesses. This amazing capacity for self-reflection and rigorous honesty leads to an increasingly accurate self-assessment. From that place they are able to make a truly authentic and unique contribution to the people around them. Becoming Level 5 means learning things you didn't even know you didn't know about yourself.

Confucius remarked, "By three methods we may learn wisdom: first, by reflection, which is noblest; second, by imitation, which is easiest; and third, by experience, which is the most bitter." In this book we have written quite a bit about the virtue of challenging experiences in our own Vertical development, but we have not stressed how important reflection is to our development. Without the ability and the time to reflect on these principles and values it is very difficult to become Level 5. Even though taking the time for reflection in our 24/7 lives may seem like a luxury, the most powerful source of renewable energy for a leader is deep personal reflection—and in today's business environment it is in short supply. A recent report found that one in three North American workers feel chronically overworked.[30] With so much daily stress there is little time for the important kind of reflection that unlocks faith, trust, courage, and other virtues necessary for leadership.

Throughout history we know great leaders have engaged in reflective practices (cf. Marcus Aurelius, *Meditations*),[31] but strangely we know less about the content of what contemporary effective leaders reflect on when making decisions. Based on our research, and in our executive coaching, leaders' reflections differ depending on their level of maturity as a leader. The content of what leaders reflect on—and also what they lose sleep over—differentiates effective from ineffective leaders.

At Level 5, leaders know that to be successful they must be more than their values. Self-awareness, coupled with a willingness to be vulnerable with others, distinguishes Level 5 leaders. We have found that Level 5 leaders reflect deeply about the best interests of the organization and how to contribute to the larger community. Level 5 leaders lead holistically: "It is not about *some* of us, but about *all* of us."

When leaders take the time to reflect on their decisions, it is their leader level that frames how those decisions are made. If you reflect from Level 5, become intentional in the development of others, and seek integration of your ideas with others, then you are likely leading with greater maturity and effectiveness.

How Level 5 Leaders See Others

Level 5 leaders understand the inherent value of others. Sure, there is the benefit of personal growth as a side effect when you begin to focus on others, but there is also a larger realization. As Karl just stated, life is not just about some of us; it's about all of us. It's not just about you; it's about you and me in relationship to one another. It's not just about your organization or group; it's about everyone's organizations and groups. It's not just about your generation; it's about the commonalities held across generations

We can't read the first-person writings of Dr. Martin Luther King, Jr., or Abraham Lincoln, or Gandhi, or Mother Teresa—all Level 5 leaders—and not marvel at their ability to consistently be "other-focused." Even in the midst of their incredibly challenging circumstances, they weren't overly concerned about the maintenance of their own welfare or their way of accomplishing a task (which are the priorities of a Level 4 leader). Rather, they were motivated to an extreme extent by the growth and welfare of others, whether individuals or society as a whole. Paradoxically, by acting on what they saw through their selfless lens, their influence and stature increased. They became great by serving the growth needs of others.

In Dr. Martin Luther King, Jr.'s *Letter from Birmingham Jail*,[32] we see the power of viewing the world this way. King realized that the differences between the black clergy and the white clergy were not simply positions that needed to be reconciled, but rather two positions that informed each other in search of a better whole. Through the lens of a higher-order ethic, King was able to understand the perspective of the white clergy as well as the perspective of his own group affiliations. In other words, he was able to meet the other where the other was, and in doing so he better understood where *he* was. He was able to evaluate two differing approaches to nonviolence (active and passive) in a way that transformed how both groups understood the situation.

In contrast, many other groups of the civil rights era were trying to manage the differences between the various constituencies. King's Level 5 understanding enabled him to recognize what the opposing perspectives had in common and leverage the differences between the two groups in pursuit of a greater good. Through the higher-order lens of freedom and equality, Dr. King was able to weave the beauty of diversity into a cohesive tapestry. He made sense of ethical and cultural differences in a way that promoted hope. In leadership development terms, he met the nation where she was and led her closer to where he was.

A Level 2 perspective would insist that one group win and one group lose. A Level 3 perspective would require that we all just get along. A Level 4 perspective would focus on managing our differences effectively. But from the unique perspective of Level 5, differences are appreciated and leveraged toward the achievement of our common interests. A Level 5 leader sees others as fellow sojourners in life and how we are all inexorably bound by our need for one another. Without each other, none of us can continue to grow. As King wrote in the *Letter from a Birmingham Jail*, "We are caught in an inescapable network of mutuality, tied in a single garment of destiny."

These same servant-leader behaviors exist in Level 5 leaders of companies. Their success is the result of their capacity to rise above established organizational patterns of leadership, communication, vision, and performance. Through a Level 5 lens, they make sense of complex circumstances and create a culture that nurtures the growth of the people who work for them. Ironically, we usually don't hear about these leaders in the press because they tend to shun the spotlight. But we hear of their outstanding companies, and we hear from the employees they've influenced. We see the effectiveness of their influence through the sustainability of their organizations.

Jim Collins has done significant and thorough research to identify the key attributes of organizations that consistently outperform others in any given industry and across industries. He shares his insightful conclusions in his book, *Good to Great*.[33] He says one feature great organizations have in common is the type of leaders who run their operations. (Collins calls them Level 5 leaders, but note that he is measuring behavior—a way of acting. We have been using the term to describe a way of understanding ourselves, others, and the world around us—a way of knowing. Still, there are great similarities between the descriptions of Collins's Level 5 leaders and the Level 5 profile presented in this chapter.) Collins notes that Level 5 leaders displayed, among other things, humility, a concern for others and the institution above themselves, and a deliberate investment in the development of others.

The Level 5 Leader

One of the best examples of a Level 5 leader in my own experience is Henry. I met Henry in his office at his company's corporate complex in a small, New England college town. At the time of our interview, Henry worked for a company we will call Health Systems, Incorporated. HSI was a growing, publicly held company in the health care management industry. (A huge conglomerate acquired the company for over a billion dollars in the mid-2000s.) Although the company had offices in larger cities across the country, I had the sense that continuing to be headquartered in this small remote town was about values and quality of life both for the leaders and the workforce.

Henry was around sixty years old at the time of the interview and had been working for HSI for about three years, but he had been associated with the CEO/founder for twenty years as one of HSI's first clients. As Chief Operating Officer, Henry's role demanded leadership in operationalizing a rapidly growing organization working toward the achievement of its objectives. Others whom I interviewed at the same company described him as brilliant, thorough, analytical, and deliberate. He had a remarkable ability to see and evaluate all sides of any problem, and if there was any frustration with his leadership, it was that he was perceived as being too deliberate and not decisive enough. This is a common criticism directed toward Level 5 leaders. Their willingness to fully meet others where they are, including making sure the other feels understood, is sometimes perceived as uncertainty or indecision.

HSI provided cutting-edge technology in healthcare software. They had in many ways revolutionized the way doctors and hospitals collected data to better serve patients through computerized information management. HSI experienced an exponential amount of growth during Henry's tenure with them, and Henry stayed on with HSI for another four years before returning to the university and his practice as a physician.

Henry had more or less stumbled into his career while a young physician in the Armed Forces. He was assigned to a project to improve the ways doctors and patients interacted so that diagnoses would be more effective. At that time the technology wasn't ready for easily computerized records, but Henry's team created algorithms for people to use in the field: if certain symptoms were present, then corpsmen would take diagnostic steps for care. Among the results of his efforts were a bestselling book and a training program for the Army. In addition, the Army discovered it really did need to develop a computerized medical record system. And Henry learned that, "If you have a vision, it doesn't have to be specific at the very beginning. . . . The vision gets built in pieces, and you have to be ready to accept changes to achieve that vision as you go along."

When Henry left the Army in 1970, he attributes to "luck" the fact that his successor had a good friend ("a genius in medicine") in the Northeast who was looking for a way to computerize the records at a medical school. After reviewing Henry's Army experience and hearing his goals to streamline the way doctors took care of patients, the friend hired Henry. The university had a plan in place to hire fresh new graduates and bring them along, but Henry instinctively felt it would take less time to hire experienced doctors who already acknowledged the need for change. In spite of their objections, Henry followed his own intuition and had soon built a 300-doctor group devoted to a more structured approach to healthcare. Their system of organizing and sharing patient records was written up in the *Wall Street Journal*.

I asked Henry about having his vision challenged. He said, "Never is your vision exactly the same year after year. You clarify it by the events that happen around you. As long as you know what it is that you want to accomplish, you're prepared when those sorts of jogs in the road come, and you're prepared to incorporate other people and new ways of thinking into your vision. If you say, 'This is the only thing I can do, and I can only do it this way,' you put your vision at high risk."

I pressed Henry to see how he felt about actively seeking out contradictions and challenges to what he believed to be best. He thought that in most cases major commitments such as a company's vision and mission should remain steadfast. He conceded that challenges, even when they don't change the vision, can inspire a change in, or additions to, current strategies as the vision is better understood and/or expanded. But he added, "You can always find things that challenge your vision—people with different visions, different missions in the same business. It doesn't do well to change your strategies every week, but I think what I'm really examining most of the time is the way I'm trying to get there and how I see the vision being realized and actualized—what it really means to our customers."

One Level 5 CEO told me, "I think conflict is a very positive, very desirable component of the corporate culture." He's not alone. In every Level 5 interview I have conducted, conflict is viewed as a value more than a problem that needs to be managed. In Level 4 interviews, leaders may see the value in conflict, but they invest their energies in managing it.

You can hear in Henry's words an understanding of conflict that is values-oriented. The Level 5 lens, characterized by openness, embraces the tension inherent in conflict, a tension those at previous levels are bent toward solving as soon as possible.

Henry saw the benefit of conflict in a business setting. He told me, "Conflict is absolutely critical, but if not addressed it becomes absolutely debilitating. You have to have people who challenge ideas, who challenge directions, who counter prevailing views, who see the world differently, who see the way it plays out differently, who see actions differently. And an organization has to be able to take in that difference of opinion. The leadership then might decide to reject it: 'I thank you, end of conflict, end of discussion.' Or they can decide that the newly proposed option is a better way and they ought to change the way they're doing it. So conflict is always around, but sometimes the only way things get done is if we have consensus. A leader's job is to say, 'Is this a case where I have to identify the common ground?'"

Level 5 leaders know that to be successful, they must be more than their values. That is, they know who they are as leaders but are open to new ways of contributing to the common good. Self-awareness, coupled with a willingness to be vulnerable with others, distinguishes Level 5 leaders. We've found that Level 5 leaders reflect deeply about the best interests of the organization and how to contribute to the larger community.

Before Henry made executive decisions, he invited the input of others. In fact, employee surveys showed that eighty-five percent of the people at HSI believed the senior management valued their feedback. Henry said, "Willingness to listen to my people and seek out differences of opinion not only changes me, it brings them along too. So what I have tried to do is to create an atmosphere in which nobody's afraid to challenge us about our decisions and what we've done, because that feedback is critical not just for us, but for them and the whole organization."

Only in interviews with Level 5 leaders have we routinely heard people comment that being open to feedback has a positive impact on the growth of *others*. At lower levels, people are focused on how every situation and decision benefits them or the organization, not others.

Henry is at a place in his Vertical journey where the insights of others are probably not new thoughts to him. He may be better at giving himself feedback because of his Level 5 ability to take an objective view of himself. However, his willingness to receive feedback is a model for the people at other levels. His example shows them how to be open, honest, and grateful for input themselves. If you, like Henry, can take on other people's feedback and show respect for them, then you can make greater strides than you or the world might otherwise imagine.

One of the best things about Henry's interview is that we get a look into how a Level 5 leader thinks about and understands business circumstances that are relevant to the situations and challenges faced by those of us at lower levels of Vertical development. Understanding the thinking of a Level 5 leader is sometimes difficult because so few examples get highlighted, even in the abundance of literature on leadership. Most of us probably know a few Level 5 people, but in relationships that are more personal than business oriented, we don't often hear their insights in the context of business leadership.

The benefit to having access to Henry's Level 5 understanding is that regardless of your current location on the Vertical journey, you can begin to emulate and employ Level 5 behaviors from your own level of understanding. For instance, Level 3 leaders can work hard to identify and commit to values they don't want to compromise, and they can intentionally evaluate their actions against those values even in the face of outside sources pushing in a different direction. Such an effort will allow them to get beyond Outside-In understanding and put the focus instead on what they want to stand for from the inside out.

Level 4 leaders can intentionally practice Henry's behavior of listening to what others really need and seeking to meet them where they are so they can do their jobs more effectively, achieve an objective, or just keep growing. This requires discipline, and it may feel awkward at first. Many Level 4 leaders don't listen in a way that connects them with the developmental needs of others. The way they make sense of things is usually correct, so more often than not they will just solve the problem or tell others what to do to fix it rather than focus on developmental opportunities behind the problem. However, in developing the Level 5 skill of listening in this new way, Level 4 leaders can begin to see the commonality of values that tie people together, and they will potentially gain a new self-awareness that allows a more objective view of their own way. It will also minimize the tendency to arrest their development due to the success that has resulted from their self-authored understanding.

> As I stated earlier, reflection is the inner work of leadership. Being reflective doesn't detract from decisiveness. In fact, reflection helps prepare for the difficult choices that great leaders must make. When we reflect like Level 5 leaders, we become intentional in the development of others. We seek integration of our ideas with others, and we knit together our differences through the lens of what we have in common. When we reflect through this Level 5 prism, we lead with greater maturity and increasing effectiveness.

The effectiveness of Level 5 leaders is markedly greater than that of Level 4 leaders. Experts in leadership effectiveness have evaluated various leader level responses to a series of leadership situations.[34] They found Level 5 responses more effective than any of the lower level responses in dealing with leadership issues like complexity, conflict, motivation, change, and developing others, to name a few. At Level 5, there is an others-focused, big-picture, greater-good orientation to the responses.

Moving On

Robert Greenleaf was an early proponent for the concept of servant leadership. After a number of years at AT&T in the mid-1900s, he became frustrated with the traditional authoritarian model of leadership. He retired early and started the Greenleaf Center for Servant Leadership. He acknowledged the difficulty of measuring effectiveness when it comes to servant leadership. He wrote, "The best test, and difficult to administer, is this: Do those served grow as persons?

Do they, *while being served*, become healthier, wiser, freer, more auton-
omous, and more likely themselves to become servants?"[35]

By comprehending the Map for Vertical development, we come
closer to understanding servant-leaders, measuring their achievement
of servant-leadership, and seeing why Greenleaf's two questions are
important. True servant leaders, at Level 5, engage in behaviors that
allow and even facilitate Vertical development in others.

> The Level 5 approach has an inherent authenticity and
> vulnerability. Its degree of honesty promotes a perspective
> where the achievement of a valued end state is necessar-
> ily bigger than any individual leader or any individual way.
> Level 5 values lead to a more generative, sustainable, and
> enduring legacy—for an organization, a family, a culture, or
> even a nation.

It is rare to find someone who understands the Vertical development Map who doesn't desire to someday become Level 5. When
we meet a real Level 5 leader, most of us instinctively crave the wisdom, effectiveness, broader perspective, peace, humility, happiness,
and satisfaction that indicate the individual has reached his or her
Promised Land.

We have come to the end of the Map for the Vertical journey as
we know it. In our programs that help facilitate accelerated Vertical
development in others, some will ask (hopefully) tongue-in-cheek,
"How can I get to Level 6?" We respond with what we know right
now: No Level 6 has been identified. However, it's all most people can

do to learn the Map, begin to see themselves at a specific point on the journey, recognize where others are on their journeys, and intentionally accelerate developmental growth whenever possible.

In the following section, we are going to look at what we need to do in order to accelerate our own and others' development to a place of greater effectiveness, greater satisfaction, and greater influence— to make tangible, noticeable, and doable progress toward our Level 5 Promised Lands.

Consider This . . .

1. Who is the most developmentally fit person you know? Do you think this person has arrived at Level 5, or is he or she still at Level 4?

2. What are some higher-level principles that are important to you? How did you come to value them? (Family upbringing? Seeing them in someone else? Etc.)

3. At this point in your life, to what extent (if at all) have you been able to connect with other people of extremely different generations, ideologies, and cultures?

4. Have you ever worked for a Level 5 leader? If so, what makes you think so?

5. Write a paragraph to summarize what you've learned about each of the levels of development. What are the characteristics of each one, and what are some challenges that might propel a person from one level to the next?

GAINING TRACTION

Knowing the Map is a huge first step toward improving Vertical growth, but reading a map is not the same as making the journey. In these final chapters, we will zero in on how to make that journey more meaningful by accelerating Vertical growth in yourself and others. Your improved performance will yield greater satisfaction, well-being, and energy to fuel even more growth, and the ultimate result will be more effectiveness in leadership, life, and legacy.

First we will look at five principles that are applicable to all of the levels of growth. Next we will use a five-step process to help you identify your "growth gap"—your personal gateway for growth—and what you need to do to walk through it. Then we will take a close-up look at what growing means at each level so you can determine how to accelerate growth in yourself and others on your Vertical journey.

Chapter 7

BETTER TRACTION
AT EVERY LEVEL

When I was a boy, people still used paper maps. It was a fairly universal experience for kids at that time, as summer approached, to unexpectedly find Dad looking at a map sprawled out awkwardly across his lap. Immediately a sense of expectation began to develop. *Are we going on vacation? Where? When? Is it far away? I hope this year it will be Disneyland!*

Maybe you had a similar experience. Maybe not. But there's still something about perusing a map that fosters a sense of wanderlust in many people. *Hmmm. The beach isn't really that far away, and we have a long weekend coming up. Then again, we've never been to those mountains. And look! Here's the state park with the waterfall that I've heard so many people talking about.* Sometimes we don't realize how much we would like to travel, and we surely don't comprehend the number of options, until we start looking at a map.

I hope the opening chapters of this book have created a similar sense of anticipation for you. After seeing how extensive is the journey of Vertical development, my hope is that you are beginning to chomp at the bit to make some more progress at this point.

Rules of the Road: The Five Principles for Accelerating Growth

Now that we have covered the five main levels of adult Vertical growth, from this point onward I will attempt to be a bit more precise. I have said we don't jump from one level to the next in an instant. Each transition is a process—some much longer than others—so to better measure that process we use smaller increments to assess growth. For example, during the testing and interviews I conducted with the leaders mentioned in the previous section (Stan, Joe, Kate, Henry, and many others), I rated each one on a scale broken into five segments for each level. As an example, rather than assessing them "between levels 3 and 4," I would position them at 3.0, 3.2, 3.4, 3.6, 3.8, or 4.0.

It only makes sense, doesn't it? If you're driving from Salt Lake City to Las Vegas, you expect quite a bit of change as you move from one city to the next. If you pay attention during that 413-mile trip, you'll notice that the smaller towns south of Salt Lake City retain the feel of that large city while the ones just north of Las Vegas reflect the Vegas ambiance. Somewhere in between you make that subtle shift from the primary influence of the city you're leaving into the influence of the one you are approaching. Moving from one level to the next is a similar, gradual transformation.

Having said that, there are certain things you can do that will be beneficial at any of the four levels of adult development and all points in between. They are guiding principles to use on the entire trip. As you learn to apply them consistently, they will not only get you where you want to be more quickly, but will also make the trip more enjoyable.

Principle 1: Know Where You Are on the Map

Having an accurate view of your present position on the Map is critical to growing effectively. Even the newest and best GPS system can't give you reliable directions if you don't provide a starting point. Your "You Are Here" pin in the Map will (hopefully) be moving if you are continuing to grow, and you need to remain aware of your current location.

You can, with a surprising degree of accuracy, self-assess your current level. Some physicians say children going through leukemia treatments can sometimes make a better prognosis of their current condition than the doctor. When someone is in treatment with harsh chemotherapies, a suppressed immune system, and frequent blood counts that reflect widely varying results, the patient learns to gauge his own status—often before the doctor does. Sometimes the numbers on the blood count might look great but the person feels lousy, and within hours the counts drop to confirm that the patient was correct. Other times the numbers look dreadful but the person feels pretty good, and sure enough, the numbers become more robust before long.

Developmental self-assessment is much the same way. As you become more familiar with the Map, learn to understand what to expect at each level, and are honest about your progress, you become your own GPS system. Your assessment will be quite accurate in determining your place on the journey—as good or better, in most cases, than a trained professional conducting and scoring a ninety-minute interview.

After determining your current location through honest reflection of how you understand your circumstances, self, and others, from that point you make progress one small step at a time. If you determine you are at Level 3.4 for example, your next step is to become Level 3.6, not Level 5. You don't get to vault over the next stage to a place you want to be. You must pass through all the mileposts along the way.

The good news is that you need not lose heart if you determine your level is lower than you want it to be. If you are familiar with the Map and know where you are, you can put yourself on a strong path for continued accelerated growth and "catch up" much faster than you would ever expect. In my work facilitating the growth of leaders, many participants are between Levels 3 and 4. With intentional effort applied to the principles laid out in this chapter, we often see Vertical growth that would normally take eight years occur within a period of six months.

Sometimes this explosive progress is due to a pent-up demand for growth. For many people, merely understanding the Map and the importance of leaning into (rather than avoiding) challenges unleashes growth that has been corralled for years. When people are stuck for a period of time, they feel as though they have been going in circles. The clarity provided by the Map and their location, coupled with disciplined commitment to growth strategies, often leads to immediate and transformational growth traction.

Start by giving thoughtful consideration to your current location on your Vertical journey. When you understand the Map, you can consider how you understand and react to your relationships and circumstances. Do you have a me-first, have-to-win reaction when things don't go as planned? If so, you're still traveling through Level 2. Do you easily lose your sense of direction when you are in conflict with someone important to you? That sounds like a Level 3 location. Do you adhere persistently to an ideology even after new information challenges the ideology? Perhaps you've moved up to, but certainly not beyond, Level 4.

Your honest answers to questions like these can lend insight into your level. Understanding the Map is only a starting point; it is the intersection of your life with the Map that allows you to determine where you are. And once you know where you are, you can begin to make significant progress toward a higher and more effective level.

> We are often asked, "I see myself at many of these levels. Does that mean I'm sometimes Level 2, sometimes Level 3, and sometimes Level 4?" No. Remember that at any level you have access to your current level and the levels below. Even someone at Level 5 can want to excel over her competitors, but that doesn't make her Level 2. Those at Level 2 are actually limited to a me-first, winning understanding. The question is not "How low can you go?" but rather what level best characterizes the usual upper limits of your understanding.

Principle 2: Lean into the Formula for Growth

We have stated a number of times already that Vertical development from one level to the next occurs only when we face challenging circumstances that contradict our current understanding and then persevere through them until the existing tension is reconciled. This reconciliation results in a new, more complete understanding, and that new understanding is Vertical growth. The reconciliation occurs naturally over time, but that time can be intentionally reduced. We can also be intentional in identifying challenges that we might otherwise avoid or ignore. This intentionality is the underpinning of perseverance.

If we convert the Vertical growth process to a math formula, we can see the relation of the various components. We can also see how to accelerate growth in three different ways: increase the numerator C + C (Challenge and Contradiction), decrease the denominator T (Time), or increase the multiplier P (Perseverance).

Challenge and Contradiction

$$\frac{C + C}{T} \times P = VG$$

Vertical Growth

Perseverance

Time

Although Vertical growth is seldom if ever this clear-cut or mechanical, let's plug in some values just for example's sake. Start by assigning a value of one (1) to each variable. So Challenge and Contradiction (1) divided by Time (1) multiplied by Perseverance (1) results in a Vertical growth baseline of 1. If you then double the Challenge and Contradiction while the other factors remain the same, your Vertical growth is doubled. The same increased growth occurs if you double the degree of Perseverance or decrease the amount of Time by half. And if you are intentionally working on all three variables in the equation, the potential growth is greatly increased.

One of the clearest ways to increase Vertical growth, and perhaps the one over which you have most control, is the willingness to "lean into" challenging circumstances that contradict your current understanding. Challenges come in many forms. Some of them are unavoidable and involve loss: the death of a loved one, losing a job, serious health problems, and so forth. But positive events can be just as challenging: marriage, the birth of a child, a demanding new opportunity at work, etc.

In gain or loss, whether positive or negative, our challenges bump up against the inadequacy of our current understanding. After we persevere and look back, we see growth not just *through* the challenge, but *because of* the challenge. So the better you learn to embrace more of the challenging circumstances of life, the greater your rate of growth.

Leaning into challenges means you don't ignore them or sweep them under the rug. When many people begin to feel the tension created by challenge, they often ignore it or solve it, and in more destructive instances try to mask it with various types of escapism: drugs, alcohol, television, and any number of other things that only delay real growth. Leaning into challenges is the opposite of masking them.

Leaning into a challenge means that we ask ourselves some version of the question: "What can I learn new about me in these circumstances?" Even when I disagree with someone, I can consider how to stay open to hearing what is new in what he or she is saying, even when that means asking more questions and remaining longer in the conversation.

Intentionally embracing contradictions in life becomes more natural with practice. In time you even begin to identify and make the most of small challenges that would be otherwise easy to ignore, such as conflict with a colleague or disappointment with corporate strategy or direction. Embracing challenges big and small increases the numerator in the equation and accelerates growth.

You decrease the denominator (Time) by avoiding any delay in your response to challenge. Again, this happens most often when hit with one of life's painful and unavoidable challenges. For example, if you lose a job or get harsh criticism from your boss, it will consume your thinking, which actually compresses the time it takes you to work to a new understanding of the challenge. But with smaller, avoidable challenges, you must consciously hold yourself accountable to timely steps that help you deal with (lean into) the contradiction. The less intentional you are about taking steps, the more time it takes to ultimately reconcile the tension that leads to growth. Each challenge offers you the opportunity for accelerated development, but it's up to you to respond.

> The formula nudges you to consider what life would be like if you were bolder in the face of difficulties. If I were more courageous in "leaning into challenges and contradictions," would I accelerate my growth? Conversely, if I avoid conflict and challenge, would I arrest personal growth? How many people do you know who are forty-plus years of age and have tried to avoid all challenges in their life? What are they like? The ones I have known seem lost, tend to blame problems on everyone else, avoid risk, and live a very small life.

The final component of the equation is Perseverance, defined as "steadfastness in doing something despite difficulty or delay in achieving success." Vertical growth is never easy or immediate, but perseverance is the real ticket to growth. Your life can be filled with opportunities for growth through challenge and contradiction, but if you don't persevere at all, you zero out the growth equation. Masking challenges with drugs, alcohol, or some other form of avoidance also suppresses perseverance. The result is arrested development rather than growth.

Although it isn't easy or natural to lean into challenges and contradictions, choosing to do so results in Vertical growth and greater effectiveness in all aspects of life. You become a better leader, manager, and employee. You develop a more positive influence with those whose lives touch yours. Choose to embrace challenge, contradiction, and change!

It's important to be open and ready for change, but many of us are hesitant to take these steps. I wish there were a series of experiences we could prescribe for clients that would accelerate their development, but humans are more complex than a simple algorithm. Actually, it's not the experience that matters as much as how you make sense of the experience. Two people can have the same experience and take away very different lessons. A good parent, manager, friend, or counselor can help you make sense of a particular situation and use it to help you grow. This is the real value of mentors.

I had a client who had been married five times. I asked him what he had learned from his marriages. He thought for

a moment and then told me, "I'm a bad picker." My predic-
tion was there was going to be a sixth wife before long.

Principle 3: Focus on Vertical (not Lateral) Growth

To reiterate a crucial point, Vertical growth is not simply a matter
of adding to your knowledge, skills, and abilities. It's not just about
learning additional leadership behaviors. It is about becoming more
Inside-Out in your *understanding* of your knowledge, skills, and abilities. You can learn a new skill or develop new abilities at your current
level and not actually change the level. New skills or behaviors can
certainly contribute to Vertical growth, but only when they challenge
and contradict your current beliefs or what you hold to be true.

Let's look at an example. The process of managing conflict usually
involves five key steps: name the conflict, allow all parties to hear and
feel heard, identify common goals, brainstorm and evaluate solutions,
and commit to next steps. Any intelligent middle-schooler is capable of learning and employing these behaviors, but his *understanding*
will likely continue to be based on a me-first, my-agenda, Level 2 lens.
Someone at Level 3 would learn and use these skills primarily to avoid
conflict and get along better with others. Only with Level 4's Inside-Out
understanding could the person utilize the skills by aiming to achieve
the best solution, and by Level 5 the individual would be more oriented
toward utilizing conflict to promote the growth of others.

A conflict-resolving skill set can result in a more effective outcome in all cases, but only to the degree of what would have been
accomplished at that same level without the new skill. In other words,
learning and employing the Lateral behaviors doesn't change your

Vertical level unless it creates a contradiction to your current level of understanding. Even then it will be the reconciliation of that contradiction that leads to Vertical growth, not just adopting the new behaviors. We undergo Vertical growth when we focus on understanding the value of conflict in new and bigger ways.

Principle 4: Navigate Roadblocks and Detours by Knowing Yourself

A lot of us tend to blame a lack of growth on any number of factors, beginning with the vehicles we drive (personality, charisma, etc.), the baggage we carry (especially our counterproductive behaviors that were shaped earlier by people or situations), or our fuel supply (our developmental energy). We said as much in Chapter 1, but perhaps it makes more sense to you by now. Add to the list of excuses an IQ lower than desired, negative experiences from our formative years, a bad boss, a stifling organizational culture, time constraints, and other factors. But none of these things precludes us from Vertical growth—not even from the capacity to eventually become a Level 5 leader. Certainly, these are all factors to be considered, and they may indeed make your journey a bit more of a challenge, but very few of us are dealt a hand that prohibits significant Vertical development.

Some of the factors that appear to handicap you at certain points along the journey can benefit you at others, so the point is to keep moving forward. For example, some personality types have more difficulty than others growing from Level 2 to Level 3, but the same personality type has an easier transition from Level 3 to Level 4. For other personality types, it is the opposite. Some have personalities, behaviors, and/or experiences that make it more likely that they will arrest development at Level 4. Others have behavioral habits or unchecked idiosyncrasies that keep them loaded down with an excessive amount of baggage throughout most of the entire journey, and the extra weight can inhibit developmental progress at more than one of the levels.

However, just because you might be handicapped or disadvantaged at particular points on the Vertical journey does not mean that you can't navigate those very same points with great effectiveness. Even though your vehicle (personality) might not be as suited for a trouble-free crossing from one level to the next, you have a lot of control over other factors that can make that crossing completely doable. It's just likely that the way you make the crossing will look different from the crossing of someone who has a significantly different vehicle. A four-wheel-drive SUV can go across rough terrain that a sports car can't . . . unless efforts are made to smooth a path to accommodate the design of the sports car.

These personality differences are one reason why it is important to make the discovery of self-awareness a lifelong pursuit. Gaining greater insight into your personality preferences and intentionally seeking feedback from others can reveal the adjustments you might need to make in order to overcome potential limitations. As you do, the things you need to change to accelerate your progress will become increasingly clear.

If you have read this far, you have the ability to make the transition from any given level to the next, and you have the ability to continue Vertical development all the way to Level 5. If I went into detail on this fourth principle, it could easily fill an entire book in itself. But much is already available on the subject of personality assessment, and additional information is easily accessible through books, local professionals, and even online. It might take a little courage to pursue commonsense approaches for feedback on your baggage, but they aren't complicated. Seize every opportunity to know yourself better in order to accelerate growth from any level.

> Ask others, "What's one thing I can do differently to make you more effective?"

Principle 5: Engage in Developmental Relationships

Vertical growth is hard work that requires developing a new, more comprehensive understanding of *everything*—how you perceive your world, yourself, and others. It is possible to make the journey primarily on your own, and at times going solo is necessary due to the self-reflective requirements of growth. Yet we accelerate our growth when we include others in our efforts. Engaging others is usually most productive if the developmental relationships are reciprocal, not one-way. Even mentoring relationships are more effective when mentors share their own growth objectives with the mentee.

Much like recruiting a partner to undergo a challenging diet, train for a marathon, or start a gym workout program, enlisting others in developmental relationships creates ongoing accountability and feedback. In addition, the other person's insights and ideas can help you accelerate growth exponentially over doing it on your own. Intentional growth is never easy, but it we make it more difficult than necessary when we go it alone.

We have many types of relationships (social, work, family, friendship, romantic, etc.), each with its own distinct characteristics. The distinction of your *developmental* relationships should be to mutually share growth objectives, ask each other for ideas, and create accountability to make progress.

Ellen Van Velsor and her colleagues have researched the impact of developmental relationships in increasing our capacity for growth and have identified three types of developmental relationships: assessment relationships, challenge relationships, and support relationships. Instead of trying to grow in isolation, the general rule is "the more the merrier" in regard to accelerating growth.[36]

Assessment relationships are those with people who observe your attempts to challenge yourself in new ways toward your goals. For example, as I delegate a specific project or activity to someone on my team, I could let that person know I am doing so as part of my own development. Then I can solicit feedback: Am I too involved? Am I not supportive enough? What else does the person need from me? If I also tell my boss or a colleague what I am trying to do, that's another perspective I can get on how well I am making steps toward my goal. People in your assessment relationships have to know what you are trying to do and be close enough to the situation to see you do it.

Try to identify "next generation" leaders who can assess your efforts. Going public with your intentions not only fuels your growth, but it often accelerates their growth as well.

The second type of developmental relationship is the *challenge* relationship where you submit yourself to the accountability and feedback of people who don't have a stake in your goals or strategies (other than wanting what is best for you). Challenge relationships work best when they are reciprocal, where you can evaluate and challenge others even as they challenge you. Relationships with mentors, coaches, counselors, or just a group of colleagues can also fall into this category if we hold ourselves accountable to them and allow them to push us to make regular progress in our efforts to grow.

The third type of relationship is the *support* relationship. Sometimes our goals require significant emotional, financial, or time commitments, so the people in your support relationships provide encouragement, input, and/or resources necessary to help you deal with the tensions you will face as you try to accelerate your Vertical growth. It is wise to request the support of your boss, colleagues, or partners. Many people reach out to their spouse or close friends for support.

In all of these relationships, considering the perspectives of others enables you to gain a more complete and objective understanding of yourself. You will have more in your rearview mirror to draw from. Vertical growth is just that—the ability to move beyond the lenses of yesterday as you gain an increasingly more comprehensive current lens. It is possible to do this alone; it's just not as effective. Without a little help along the way, your growth is more likely to muddle along at a rate determined by the frequency of challenges you can't avoid or solve on your own.

Perhaps the main reason we need partners to hold us accountable is that we often don't see an accurate reflection of ourselves when we look in the mirror—we're either too easy or too hard on ourselves. We may think we see ourselves clearly, but having someone encourage us (or point out our blind spots) is essential.

In conclusion, these five principles have the capacity to change the way we think about growth. They create context and points of reference for our journeys. They turn our perspective of challenges from things that must be endured to opportunities for accelerated growth. They help us focus more on changing the way we see things and less on learning new things. They put our less changeable strengths and struggles into perspective by helping us distinguish between our vehicles (personalities) and the journey itself.

Give these principles some thought. Do you have adequate traction on your current journey? Those of us who try to get ahead of ourselves sometimes spin our wheels furiously, resulting in a lot of noise and smoke, but no progress. Others stray off track a bit and get stuck in the mud with no tow truck in sight. Use these principles to adjust your course and your pace, and then move ahead to discover what area of growth might be most beneficial to you right now.

Consider This . . .

1. Based on everything you've read so far (and possibly feedback from people who know you well), where exactly would you say you are on the Map? Don't just pinpoint a level; use the scale that breaks down each level into five segments. (See page 184.)

2. Review the growth formula from Principle 2. At this point in your journey, where would it be most beneficial for you to make an adjustment: Increase your challenges and contradictions? Decrease the time factor? Improve your perseverance? What are your initial ideas for how to make needed changes?

3. Give some thought to your recent Lateral growth as opposed to Vertical growth, and to your ability to differentiate between the values you hold and your capability to understand those values. Does your self-assessment verify your previous estimation of where you are on the Map? Explain your answer.

4. Think about your vehicle (personality, charisma, etc.), baggage, developmental energy, mental acuity, negative experiences from past years, and other factors that make you who you are. Which aspects have been handicaps to your growth in the past? Which have been (or might yet be) assets for you? In what ways?

5. What people in your life come to mind when you think of developing:

    Assessment relationships?

    Challenge relationships?

    Support relationships?

Chapter 8

IDENTIFYING YOUR GROWTH GAP

In 2013 the footwear segment of Nike had revenues of over $14.5 billion. If you add the $9.5 billion sold by Adidas and another almost $2 billion from Puma, that's $26 billion worth of shoes from the top three companies.[37] A casual observer might wonder if that doesn't sound a little excessive. Does the average person really need so many pairs of shoes?

The average person? Perhaps not. But devoted sports enthusiasts are always on the lookout for better footwear. The first time a hacker attempts an uphill chip shot from a steep muddy slope, only to have his foot slide into the pond as his ball veers off course, he is likely to soon invest in some golf shoes. When a weekend climber is dangling precariously off a rocky cliff because she can't get a decent toehold in her Keds, she will shell out some money for authentic climbing shoes before next time. Athletes in most sports will attest to the importance of decent traction—not just for peak performance, but also for essential safety.

Traction is important on your Vertical journey as well. But what do you do if you discover an area where your growth is impeded? What then?

A one-size-fits-all solution would be nice, but is not possible because everyone has a unique journey. We don't respond the same way at the various levels. Even though the Map is guiding us all to Level 5 as an ultimate destination, how we get there might vary significantly based on our specific strengths, weaknesses, and responses to challenges.

One thing that seems to be true of all of us, however, is we get stuck at points along the way. The sooner we learn to identify the source of our "stuckness" and find a way to get some traction, the sooner we get back on the track to growth again. I will get stuck at places different from you, so we need an individualized approach to identifying the problem.

Karl and I have created what we call a Growth Gap Tool to help people gain traction through this process. It is based on a model proposed by Robert Kegan and Lisa Lahey.[38] The layout of the tool is not as important as learning the steps, so grab a pen and a sheet of paper and we will begin to try to identify the challenges relevant to your unique experiences that contribute to your stuckness.

Step 1: Embrace Your Complaints

Most of us don't go a day without complaining about something. Complaints just bubble up inside of us without permission or warning, and we are unequipped to stop them. Yet complaints don't solve problems or change circumstances. One option, which we might presume is the mature one, is to suppress them like an action hero who ignores pain and distractions in order to focus on saving the world.

But ignoring or suppressing your complaints will not lead to growth. Far better is to determine what your complaints are trying to teach you. The reason we complain is because something we care about is being threatened. Complaints shed light on our values or on those things that matter most to us. I complain about bad drivers because I value things like safety, consideration, and respect. If I didn't value those things, I wouldn't complain about the person who is driving like an idiot. If I didn't care about the character of our nation, I wouldn't complain about the politicians or the decisions they make. If I didn't care about making a difference at work, I wouldn't complain about how my boss manages me.

What is one of your biggest complaints right now? What frustrates you at work? At home? With a boss, colleague, spouse? With yourself? (Most of us don't need to think about this one for very long.) Write it down:

I hate it when . . .
It would be so much better if . . .
It drives me crazy that . . .

Be completely honest and candid. Stop thinking, *Oh, I shouldn't complain about that.* Embrace your complaint because real, honest complaints are the starting point for relevant and productive growth.

Generally speaking, Level 2 complaints tend to be about loss, rule violations, and other offenses to a me-first, my-agenda, overly concrete understanding. Level 3 complaints are more about relationships being violated, which might involve not just personal matters but also relationships in regard to roles, organizations, political ideologies, and even circumstances. At both levels, complaints almost always involve blame of someone or something besides us. When understanding is Outside-In and something goes wrong, it can't really be our fault, so the blame game ensues.

From the Level 4 Inside-Out perspective, complaints tend to be more internal. We become dissatisfied about letting ourselves down in some way, or about our inability to manage relationships or time. At Level 5 we generally have fewer complaints, but when we do they are often about not achieving something bigger than ourselves—perhaps a missed opportunity to leverage circumstances for the growth of others or ourselves.

Regardless of the level, our complaints can identify our point of stuckness by acting as an internal guide to reveal the values that mean the most to us. But more importantly, they point to a gateway that will lead to Vertical growth which results in greater effectiveness, satisfaction, well-being, and energy as we accelerate our development in leading, life, and legacy.

Complaining is easy. Next comes the much harder work of examining our complaints to see what may be behind them.

> For this exercise, make sure you identify a real complaint—the kind of complaint that has really bothered you for a while, not a mere annoyance that emerged two days ago. If you have trouble coming up with one, consider this: When you come home from work and those closest to you ask how your day has gone, what difficult person or what nagging problem spills out of your mouth? You get the idea. Without an honest, candid complaint, this exercise doesn't have as much impact or potential for your growth.

Step 2: Identify Your "Bigger-Me" Values

The goal at Step 2 is to identify the values behind your complaint—not just any values, but values that will stretch you and draw you to a higher level of understanding. Think of these as "bigger-me" values.

To take Step 2 effectively, you need to have a clear comprehension of where you are on your journey of Vertical growth. If you have read this far, you probably have a pretty good idea, and your complaint should help you know for sure. Depending on your level, you will follow one of two different sets of instructions. Complaints reflecting a "being done to" by some outside source (boss, circumstances, colleagues, spouses, friends, etc.) often indicate a Level 2 or 3 position and will need to be run through the first set of instructions that follow (Outside-In). Complaints reflecting an "it's my responsibility" frustration with something (mismanagement of time, avoiding issues, getting into difficult situations, etc.) need to be run through the second set of instructions (Inside-Out).

Outside-In Instructions for Identifying Bigger-Me Values (Levels 2 and 3)

What clues does your complaint (from Step 1) provide about what really matters to you? What values have been rubbed up against or violated in some way? What do you stand for? The answer to this question probably sounds a lot like the opposite of the complaint. For example:

Complaint: "My boss is holding me back."
Step 2 Values: Getting promoted and advancing in my career.

Complaint: "My teenager is driving me crazy!"
Step 2 Values: Having an obedient and well-behaved child.

So at this point take a look at your complaint. Determine what it is that you care most about that your complaint reveals is not being fully realized—or worse, violated. On your paper, take an initial stab at finishing this sentence:

What I value or care most about is _____.

Now hold on . . . you're not finished. The fact that you have an Outside-In perspective and still depend on the input of others means that you need to go beyond a "being done to" complaint (if you haven't yet done so). The irony is that you need the help of an outside source to figure out how to not be held in place by outside sources. Your bigger-me values have to be something *you* can control, which was not the case in the previous examples. You can't force your boss to give you a promotion or your child to behave himself. So you need to revise those values.

Let your complaint stand the way it is. It has done its work. But what you now need to do is see if you can find a way to generalize your stated value so that it is not about you, but could apply as a principle. You want to make your Step 2 values about something that is bigger than you. See what a difference it makes:

Step 2 Values: Getting promoted and advancing in my career
Generalized, Bigger-Me Values: Fair promotion policies, realizing potential, advancement.

Step 2 Values: Having an obedient and well-behaved child.

Generalized, Bigger-Me Values: Compliance, respect, becoming a good citizen.

In generalizing these values, they are no longer constrained by the me-focused lens of Level 2 or the codependency of Level 3. You don't lose the thing that is truly important—what you really care about—but instead elevate that value in a way that is bigger than you.

So take a look at how you expressed *your* value and then generalize it. If you are not sure you have it right, set it aside while you go through Steps 3, 4, and 5, and then review it and edit (or add to) what you have written.

Inside-Out Instructions for Identifying Bigger-Me Values (Levels 4 and 5)

What does your complaint (from Step 1) suggest really matters to you? What values have been rubbed up against or violated in some way? What do you stand for?

If you have correctly evaluated your level as being more Inside-Out than Outside-In, both your complaint and your values should reflect Vertical maturity—you should not be blaming someone or something, but rather taking responsibility for both the complaint and the values. As we have said, "I get angry when that happens" is the Inside-Out version of "That makes me angry." The former takes responsibility while the latter blames.

Let's look at some examples stated in an Inside-Out way:

Complaint: "I'm not advancing in my career the way I want to."

Step 2 Values: Promotion or career advancement.

Complaint: "I'm driven crazy by my teenager!"
Step 2 Values: Raising great, productive, contributing kids.

Now, look again at your own complaint. What do you value or care most about that the complaint shows is not being fully realized—or worse, violated? On your paper, finish this sentence:

What I value or care most about is _____.

If you are Level 4 dominant, your stated values will beg for a better paradigm for managing your complaint effectively. Therefore, after you get your first answer, ask yourself *why* that matters to you. When you get that answer, ask yourself why again. Keep asking until you want to say, "I don't know why—that's just who I am!" Your thought process should go something like this:

Step 2 Values: Promotion or career advancement.
Why is that important? "Because I want to realize my potential."
Why is that important? "Because I want to have an impact on clients, employees, the business."
Why is that important? "I don't know. It's just important to me to lead well."
Perfect! That's a bigger-me value.

Step 2 Values: Raising great, productive, contributing kids.
Why is that important? "Because I believe it will make their quality of life better."
Why is that important? "Because I want to contribute to a better quality of life for others"

Why is that important? "I don't know. That's just how I am."

Perfect! That's a bigger-me value.

By repeatedly asking yourself "why?" you are trying to elevate your initial response to one with more impact on others, or to a purpose bigger than yourself. This elevation will be more Level 5 in nature, farther up the Vertical trajectory, thereby pulling you to a higher level of Vertical development. The initial complaint creates a relevant gateway—one that if addressed effectively should matter to you and lead to greater effectiveness. But the *why* questions do the work of elevating your values to bigger-me values.

> Producing a "bigger-me" value isn't difficult for many next-generation managers, but it's frequently a challenge for my undergraduate audience between the ages of eighteen and twenty-four because they're often Outside-In on their Vertical journey and can't articulate bigger-me values without help. If you're mentoring people at lower levels, be patient in helping them author Section 2 values that are bigger-me; don't simply tell them your bigger-me values and expect them to own them.

Step 3: Take Responsibility

You start with your complaint. You ponder and analyze it until you determine the bigger-me value that lies behind it. Now what?

In Step 3 you ask yourself what you have thought of doing that you have been reluctant to do. How could you take responsibility for more fully realizing your Step 2 Values? This step can't be about doing more of something you have already been doing, and it doesn't even need to be realistic. By the way, you don't need to worry that we are going to ask you to do what you write down. It is simply the next step to make the tool work effectively.

Go back to your paper and complete this sentence:

What I could do that I haven't done to more fully realize this bigger-me value is _____.

As we said, at this step it is important to think of something you have not done or are not currently doing—it's not a revision of something you have already tried, and not doing more of the same thing, only harder. You may have already considered this action, or perhaps you have had a hunch that you should do something, but you have been reluctant to this point. Now is the time to put pen to paper:

"I could initiate a conversation."
"I could say no to an opportunity."
"I could be stricter in my parenting."

Your proposed action may be something completely new, or even a little outrageous:

"I could jump up on a chair and demand a promotion."
"I could quit my job and find a more organized place to work."
"I could send my child away to boarding school."

What you wrote down—the idea of what you could do that you are not currently doing—should create a bit of a pit in your stomach.

Any relevant new idea for taking responsibility will result in a little anxiety—maybe a lot! We worry because things could go wrong in some way, we might be ostracized, or we might fail. You will address your worries at the next step, so here you need to resist any temptation to jump to the most convenient answer that seems to resolve your complaint. This step is your opportunity to identify not the solution to your complaint, but rather to highlight the anxiety that may be keeping you stuck. If you solve the complaint, you steal your opportunity to use it for growth. Make the most of the opportunity your complaint provides while you have it.

> People usually don't have much problem identifying a number of new things they might try to address their problem. Frequently the bigger challenge is for them to acknowledge the *one thing* they already know they *aren't* doing! For this exercise, focus on the first thing that comes to mind. At this stage being honest with yourself is more important than taking action. Keith pointed out that a lot of participants want to immediately run out and do whatever it is that they wrote down, but to do so would only resolve their problem at the same level of Vertical thinking rather than enabling them to grow to a new one.

Step 4: Name Your WFRs (Worry, Fear, or Resistance)

If the action you proposed in Step 3 raised a sense of worry, fear, or resistance, you're on the right track. Step 4 is the time to name that specific concern. It should be something you don't want to happen—the dark hidden obstacle lurking in the back of your mind that has kept you from acting already. Some examples might be helpful:

Step 3 Responsibility: "I could initiate a conversation."
Step 4 WFR: "I could be uncomfortable, embarrassed, or even rejected."

Step 3 Responsibility: "I could be stricter in my parenting."
Step 4 WFR: "It could backfire and my relationship with my child would be even worse."

On your paper, underneath your Step 3 action, write down your Step 4 worry, fear, or resistance. You know what you could do to more fully realize the bigger-me values, so what's keeping you from doing it?

I suspect that in many cases your first draft may be a somewhat sanitized version of what you're really afraid of—perhaps what you might be willing to share in a group. But if you are truthful, many times your WFRs are bigger and badder than you let on— worst-case scenarios. They are the fears that race through your mind at bedtime and wake you up at 3:00 a.m.:

"I could get fired and at my age I might not find another job."
"I won't be able to pay my mortgage."
"This relationship could completely dissolve."
"My child might leave and never speak to me again."

What's a worst-case scenario for your specific challenge? If something comes to mind, write it down.

This step of naming your WFRs can be powerful. By naming them you minimize the potential they have to paralyze you from taking actions that might improve your situations and circumstances.

WFRs also reflect our level of growth in much the same way our complaints do. If your WFRs are about not winning or getting your way, they may point to Level 2. If they are about how others might view you, or about circumstances defining you in a way you won't be able to make sense of, they may point to Level 3. If, on the other hand, your WFRs are more Inside-Out in nature (perhaps about letting yourself down in some way), they may point to Level 4. You will still have WFRs even at Level 5, but they are often about missing an opportunity for growth—for yourself or someone else.

Your worries, fears, and resistance are not a foolproof assessment of Vertical development, but they are another piece of data that can help you understand where you are on the Map. When you take time to really think about the WFRs you wrote down, real life has a way of intersecting with your thoughts and highlighting the truth.

The worry, fear, or resistance holding you back from doing what you know you could be doing is not hard to identify—hard to admit to, for sure, but not hard to identify. A few general classes of worry, fear, or resistance often show up. These include: "I am not really good enough to pull this off;" "I will be deemed a non-team player;" "I will be isolated;" or "I will be seen as a troublemaker." All of these fears are real to an extent, but at this point in the exercise the goal is simply to identify and acknowledge what is holding you in place.

Step 5: Identify Your "Smaller-Me" Values

Your worries, fears, and resistance are things you usually tend to avoid. Who wants to be ostracized, minimized, or fired? Who wants important relationships to dissolve or be put at risk? Who willingly invites embarrassment or discomfort? Sometimes we go to great lengths trying to protect ourselves from the potential consequences connected with our WFRs, especially when we envision a worst-case scenario.

Step 5 begins with two questions, the easier one first. Review your responses to Step 4, and then write your answer to this question:

What do you do to protect yourself from your Step 4 WFRs?

List all the self-protective behaviors or strategies you use to keep from having to experience your worry, fear, or resistance. For example:

"I keep my mouth shut and my head down."

"I say yes to everything."

"I put up with the status quo."

"I grin and bear it."

"I work harder or longer."

"I ignore it."

What do *you* do? Write it down.

Most people don't need much time to answer this first question, but take all the time you need before moving on. Once you have your answer, you can move on to the second question in Step 5 where the tougher work begins. Review what you just wrote down and then write the answer to this question:

What do these self-protective behaviors tell you that you might also value?

The answer to this second question is usually not something we are eager to share publicly. You arrived at your bigger-me values at

Step 2, but your answer to this question will be your "smaller-me" values. They will most likely reflect concern about your reputation, comfort, or safety. Virtually no one is proud to broadcast:

"I'm committed to maintaining the status quo."

"It's really all about me."

"I think I'm better than you."

"I put career advancement above my family."

"I need to be liked."

In fact, a good rule of thumb is that if you aren't a little embarrassed, ashamed, or creeped-out by what you write, you need to look at yourself a bit closer and be more honest. Smaller-me values describe who you currently are. They impede your progress because when bolstered by your worries, fears, or resistance, they are a strong adversary to the bigger-me person you want or need to be in order to keep growing Vertically.

These Step 5, smaller-me values should be in tension with your Step 2, bigger-me values—and that's the whole point. It is identifying the contradiction between the two that enables you to identify your gateway for Vertical growth.

This smaller-me value is who you are, too. Who doesn't care about their position in the organization, paying their mortgage, or getting along with others? The point of this step is to accept the fact that you are this smaller value too—but not to let it define you. For many of us, this smaller-me identification becomes a default value—"background music," so to speak—if we aren't careful. If what you really care about is maintaining your position in the company and "not rocking the boat," there's a good chance you'll never get around to what is most important to you—your stated value in Step 2. What is at stake is never living into your destination.

If you're leading a team, and the team thinks you only care about your position (smaller-me value) and not what's in the best interest of the organization, it's unlikely you'll have much influence with them . . . let alone successfully lead the enterprise. The point for all of us is to accept the smaller-me value and know it's holding us in place. It challenges what's most important to us in Step 2, our bigger-me value.

Your GO Statement

As you evaluate what you wrote down on your paper, Steps 2 and 5 should contradict each other—or at minimum be in tension with one another. If you reconcile this contradiction or tension, however, you should see that you will have a different capacity to address the complaint that started this whole process in Step 1. In fact, when you are able to reconcile the tension or contradiction between Steps 2 and 5, you will probably have outgrown the complaint.

Growth always occurs when we are faced with challenges we can't avoid. When life puts unavoidable challenges in our path, we *have* to grow Vertically as we reconcile whatever tension the challenge creates. What this five-step process provides is a conflict that you can reconcile if you so choose. The very reason you had a complaint to start with is that you have avoided the challenge so far.

Are you ready to stop avoiding and start reconciling on purpose? By using these steps intentionally to lean into an otherwise *avoidable* challenge and tension you will grow into a new and better under-standing. Isn't it worth it? If not, you will be ceding your growth to the *unavoidable* whims of circumstances. You may not stop growing, but more people than not eventually do. The way to avoid arresting your development is through intentionality and perseverance. This tool, the Growth Gap Tool, is a learnable, repeatable way to make sure this doesn't happen.

Once you have your Growth Gap Tool (these five steps) to a point where you feel you have captured something true about the tension that may be holding you in place, you can use it to create a Growth Objective (GO) Statement. This exercise will help you take small steps and gain further insight into the tension. Spell out your GO Statement by completing the following sentence:

> "During the next year I want to become better at [insert your bigger-me values] and not be held in place by [insert your smaller-me values]."

Don't overthink your GO Statement. The shorter and more memorable, the better. You want a high-level, aspirational, but directional statement. It should be broader than the specifics of work or home, and should have application in both.

Finally, you should be able to take responsibility for the entire GO Statement (both what you want to become, and what's holding you in place). Remember, it's the tension that fuels growth. A statement that reads, "During the next year I want to be promoted, and not be held in place by my small-minded boss" is not good because you don't have control of either segment. A better example would be: *During the next year I want to be better at realizing my potential to contribute, and not be held in place by maintaining the status quo.* In that case you can take responsibility for both segments. Get the idea?

On our website (www.LeadersLyceum.com/MAP/GGT) we have included several effective Growth Gap Tools and their corresponding GO Statements from real people.

Once you feel you have your GO Statement, you're ready to start creating small, measurable steps that can give you insight into the tension reflected in your GO Statement. These are seven- to fourteen-day specific actions that intuitively seem like reasonable starting points. For example:

- *By next Thursday I will ask my boss what she thinks is my biggest opportunity for growth.*
- *In the next week I will schedule a lunch with myself to identify two ways I could help my team be more effective.*
- *During the next two weeks I will have a fifteen-minute phone call with my unemployed brother-in-law to find out how his job search is going.*

I hope you can see that each one of these small steps is specific (Who? What? Where? When?), measurable (Did you do it? Yes or no?), and leans into the tension of the GO Statement: *Over the next year I want to be better at realizing my potential to contribute, and not be held in place by maintaining the status quo.* At the end of each step (preferably in a developmental relationship) you could ask yourself, *What did I learn new about myself in relationship to my GO Statement?* Every time you're able to answer that question, you're more Inside-Out than you were before you answered it. That's how intentional

Vertical growth takes place. I hope you can also see that each of the small steps will potentially and likely lead to another small step that will allow you gain even more insight into yourself and your GO Statement.

> Don't become frustrated if your small step doesn't immediately result in a positive outcome. Keep at it, or even change the small step. The key is pushing up against the tension. The worst thing to do is to take too big a step that would result in realizing the big, bad version of your worry, fear, or resistance. Rather, small steps need to shed a clarifying light on the anxiety that holds you in place and increase your chances to grow your level and your leadership.

Small steps repeated over the course of weeks and then months create a cadence for growth, and Vertical development happens. On purpose!

Now, with your GO Statement in hand, let's get specific about strategies for moving from each level to the next.

Consider This . . .

1. Now that you've walked step by step through the process of determining a significant growth opportunity, try it again with a different complaint. Review the material for each step as often as you need to.

2. Step 1: What is your complaint?

3. Step 2: What "bigger-me" value can you determine that lies behind your complaint?

4. Step 3: What is one thing you could try to realize that value— something you've been reluctant to do?

5. Step 4: What is the worry, fear, or resistance that makes it difficult for you to try your new idea?

6. Step 5: In what way(s) do you try to avoid the WFRs in this process, and what does that reveal about your "smaller-me" values?

7. As you contrast your bigger-me value with your smaller-me value, what growth opportunity does that reveal? In other words, what's your GO Statement?

Chapter 9

FROM LEVEL 2 TO LEVEL 3: WHO DO YOU TRUST?

A new word has been making the rounds in recent years: *manolescent.* It's just what it sounds like—an adolescent mentality in an adult male body. Women are generally advised to avoid such men in the dating pool, but some can't seem to resist. A related term that has been around a bit longer is the *Peter Pan syndrome,* named after the J.M. Barrie character, but typifying a concept tracing back to Roman mythology. Peter Pan didn't want to grow up, and he counted on Wendy Darling to take care of him. Today many Wendys willingly choose to care for the Peter-Pan adult males in their lives, but their initial desire to nurture soon devolves into enabling or codependency.

As we consider developmental growth, we need to make a clear distinction between behaviors that are *childlike* and those that are *childish.* Childlike behavior can be truly endearing. We try to keep our kids from growing up too fast. We want them to enjoy the innocence of youth and the sense of wonder that comes from blowing dandelion seeds on the wind or watching a butterfly emerge from its chrysalis. We hope they will carry some of that fascination of discovery with them throughout life.

Peter Pan was childlike. Adults exhibiting Level 2 behavior are childish. There's nothing endearing about people in their late twenties or beyond clinging to their me-first, my-agenda mentality, oblivious to the fact that all their peers have long since seen the world through a different lens. Certainly, we think, they will run into circumstances that challenge this Level 2 understanding. Most people do and grow into a more effective understanding, but in some cases they don't change, or they refuse to change, and growth arrests.

Growth is never easy. At every level, we get comfortable with the way we understand the world. Whenever we let go of one way of seeing things and start to grow, we feel destabilized for a while. We give up the firm footing of what we know and risk something quite different, and it takes time for that new perspective to feel natural. For most people the challenges that contradict their current understanding create more discomfort than the sense of destabilization, so they are ultimately motivated to grow.

> The real challenge to Vertical growth is that we hold assumptions about how the world works, and we don't challenge those assumptions until we have to. It's like breaking off a relationship or losing a job. We operate with a default setting, and we stay there until the operating system is changed. The late writer David Foster Wallace told a funny story that captures the problem of growth very well. Let me paraphrase it:

> Two young fish swim along, and they happen to meet an older fish swimming the other way, who nods at them and says, "Morning, boys. How's the water?" The two young fish swim on for a while, but eventually one of them looks over at the other and asks, "What the hell is water?"[39]
>
> The fundamental problem for Level 2 leaders is that they're unaware of the assumptions that hold them in place, unaware of their level, unaware of the water all around them. The challenge for such leaders is becoming aware of their assumptions and arriving at a better way to understand their world.
>
> If you're the fish, you don't want to be the last to know you're swimming in water.

Three pieces must be in place in order for us to grow, regardless of our level. First, challenges need to meet us at our current level of understanding. Second, motivation to grow to the next level happens only when the benefits of growing outweigh the consequences of not growing—if we can tolerate the consequences of not growing, we don't grow. Third, we must actually let go of our current understanding to create a new understanding that reconciles or accounts for the contradiction that the challenge created.

In growing from Level 2 to Level 3, these three points play out like this: (1) Challenges need to intersect with (and contradict) the concrete, win-lose, Level 2 understanding; (2) The person needs to see the shortcomings of insisting on his own agenda all the time as well as the benefit of acknowledging others' opinions, and be motivated to change; and (3) He needs to let go of the old me-first orientation in order to acquire the new other-coordinated orientation. As we stated earlier, Level 2 people can't skip Level 3 and go straight to Level 4, so the desired shift isn't to move from Outside-In thinking to a self-authored, Inside-Out understanding of the world. That comes later. At this point the goal should be to question one's concrete, me-first mindset and move up to collaborative, co-defined (but still Outside-In) Level 3 understanding.

We see this transition when children develop naturally from Level 2 to Level 3 during their early teenage years to their early twenties. They begin to leave behind their me-first way of seeing the world as they learn how to empathize with others and perceive the world from another person's perspective (Level 3 characteristics). For the majority of people reading this book, your transition happened during those years, so the focus of this chapter will not be on your own *personal* growth from Level 2 to Level 3, but rather how you (as parents, bosses, or coworkers) can help someone else who has been slow to make that transition. If you are someone at Level 2 who happens to be reading this book to facilitate or accelerate your growth, I applaud your efforts. You are an extremely rare exception who is either incredibly proactive or have been coerced by someone else to read this.

Parents with Children at Level 2

Let's start with parents. You probably don't need to be reminded that Level 2 understanding is a concrete, overly simplistic, black-and-white understanding of the world. You likely see it in most every heated discussion or argument. In order to provide challenges that contradict that lens, you need to allow (or create) challenges that are more complex and give-and-take, that demand attention to *our* agenda (not just *their* agenda).

Parents, one sure way to postpone the growth of your teenagers or young adults is to always protect them from reaping the consequences of their me-first behavior. If you allow them to fail a test because "I didn't feel like studying," you've created a growth opportunity. If you stand firm and ground them from a major event after they break curfew because "I didn't realize it was so late," they're likely to be more aware of the hour next time. In both cases a potential loss that can fuel growth may be realized.

Your actions will be more effective if you keep up with what's going on with school authorities and your kids' peers. Some schools are good at disciplining kids at their level by creating losses—detentions, suspensions, chores, and so forth. Maturing friends provide real-world consequences by ostracizing peers who behave in Level 2 ways when most others have begun to grow beyond this understanding. Parents need to supplement such consequences imposed by the school and peers, rather than creating a safe haven when there shouldn't be one. But if the school and peers are not holding children responsible for their actions or decisions, parents need to initiate negative consequences for them.

The consequence should be something relevant to the child. Some children respond to a temporary withdrawal of favor or approval, an expression of disappointment, or even reasoning with them at their level. For others it may take grounding, additional chores, or removal of privileges to create a significant loss. Personality preferences such as introversion and extroversion, intelligence, number of friendships, how easily they are embarrassed, or how much they want to fit in are all relevant factors in determining consequences. You may need to use totally different strategies for different children, but you need to be thoughtful about meeting each one where he or she is. This is a tough balance, and erring too much on either side (support or consequences) can be harmful, but parents who consistently err on the side of shielding the natural consequences do their children no favors regarding continued growth.

My first three kids couldn't be more different. The first responded well to being grounded and experiencing our disapproval; the second could be reasoned with and convinced why what he did was wrong; and the third required spankings when he was younger, and then grounding combined with additional undesirable chores as he entered his teenage years. I can't wait to see what it will be like with number four, because I can already tell (at age twelve) that she's different from the other three.

My kids have all attended preparatory schools with fairly affluent families, and it's astounding to hear stories of parents who actually resist or remove consequences for their kids that the school is rightfully trying to enforce. In many instances the parents of a little hellion have marched into the principal's office to have a punishment lessened or retracted. As my children's classmates grew into teenagers, it was easy to see whose parents inappropriately withheld or removed consequences because by high school many me-first, what-I-want behaviors tend to become public and potentially dangerous. Those kids haven't realized they are part of a larger fabric of family, community, and society—aspects of an increasingly Level 3 understanding.

Trying to facilitate Vertical growth in a college-age or young-adult child who is still operating from Level 2 is even more complicated for parents. Because we love our kids, it's tempting to think they will grow up fine if we protect them from difficult challenges that will contradict their understanding, but the longer they stay at Level 2, the bigger and more devastating the consequences need be to create developmental growth.

If young adult children continue to make sense of the world at Level 2, it becomes impractical and inappropriate to ground or spank them. Sometimes reasoning or being more vocal in our disapproval can work, but more often we need to stand back and do nothing as they suffer the consequences of their Level 2 behavior—refusing their requests to provide something they want, and not bailing them out of tough circumstances (sometimes even jail). The parental will-power required to make this difficult choice, and the commensurate heartache that accompanies it, is dramatically increased when the parents are at Level 3 because from that level our kids' performance still defines us, at least in part, from the outside in.

Regardless of the emotional trauma on us as parents, we need to remember that in the long run, remaining at Level 2 will be worse for our children than any temporary difficulties they, or we, must undergo to realize developmental growth.

Some parents have strange definitions of "love." Actually, people at each developmental level may have very differ- ent definitions. If parents are at the lower levels (Levels 2 or 3), the children are a reflection of them, so love means, "I appreciate you when you make me look good." How many out-of-control parents do we come across at our children's athletic events, where the child's performance appears to be more about the parent than the child? The child's success or failure actually defines the parent's identity and reputation. At higher levels of development, parents' love is about creating challenging opportunities for their children, while also ensuring support for them should they fail.

The key to growing strong and independent kids is finding the right mixture of challenge and support for each one. At a local United States Tennis Association event I attended, the regional director shared results from a survey of youth tennis players. Not surprisingly, their most stressful time was the car ride home after a tournament. Undoubtedly, the tension on the ride home is more often about the parent's disappointment than the child's loss of a match.

Dealing with Adults at Level 2

As you might suppose, interactions with adults who are arrested at Level 2 are even more difficult than with a teenager or young adult child. By that time, their behaviors are much more established—set in cement, so to speak. They have learned to filter the complexities of life through a very simplistic lens, so it is naturally harder to reason with them. Another difficulty is that we don't have a lot of practice dealing with adults as though they are middle-schoolers. But the process is the same. We need to meet them where they are, using concrete losses to help them see the weakness in their oversimplified, me-first positions and concrete rewards for gaining a more collaborative and empathetic understanding of others and the world.

If they don't initially respond, we need to determine a loss that will meet them where they are. Such consequences might include isolation, removal from a team or project, withholding promotion, a cut in pay, being denied a bonus, or the threat of firing, demotion, or lawsuit. It's no different than threatening to ground overly self-centered teenagers who refuse to change their behavior. Imposed consequences can challenge and contradict how they are making sense of the world, and over time, will potentially allow them to grow to the next level.

> When trying to help Level 2 adults grow in the workplace, we need to be more concrete than we may believe is necessary—ambiguity only confuses them. Concepts, theories, and intangibles aren't yet real for Level 2 people, so appealing to their sense of vision, mission, and impact is too abstract for their level of understanding.
>
> As you mentor Level 2 leaders, clearly identify the rules of the "growth game" and the consequences for not playing. Create wins for growing and losses for maintaining the status quo.

The ongoing goal when working with individuals at Level 2 is to convince them to empathize and see the world through the eyes of another. Try to meet them where they are and help them realize the "win" in this situation is their personal development. This win could just be keeping their job or perhaps getting to the next level in the organization, but meeting them where they are, even as we try to move them, is critical.

I coached one Level 2 guy I'll call Bob who worked in a small professional services firm. The firm's owner was a compassionate guy who decided to invest in Bob rather than fire him. He and I first brain-stormed what consequences would best intersect with Bob's Level 2 understanding, and then the owner told Bob that unless he agreed to work on his development with me as his coach, promotion would not be an option, firing was likely, and a good referral was out of the question. I was in cahoots to reinforce this "consequence" message and convince Bob that his only "win" in this situation was to work with me and start making some changes. But we had to start where Bob was—an adult with the me-first understanding of a middle-schooler. (We'll get back to Bob in a moment.)

It's one thing if you have positional authority over the Level 2 person—and even then the challenge of promoting Level 2 to Level 3 growth is hard enough. But it can be even more difficult when the person you want to help grow is a colleague, and more challenging still if it is your boss . . . or your spouse (or roommate) . . . or your parent. In such cases, creating consequences that intersect with their Level 2 understanding is not only practically difficult, but often emotionally traumatic as well. It may reach the point where the only consequence you have at your disposal is threatening to leave, or actually leaving, the organization or relationship. Even then, the other person might not change.

A forty-six-year-old business owner came to one of our programs and accurately identified himself at Level 2 when we presented the developmental Map. This realization scared the heck out of him. He ran his business as well as his family in a super-controlling, win-or-lose way. He wanted to change, but he couldn't. When the business began to crater and his wife eventually took the kids and left him, those challenges created meaningful consequences he really didn't want to suffer. The losses should have contradicted his overly simplistic lens of maintaining order and "winning" by categorically assigning roles and lines of authority. Yet he was still unable to change his Level 2 understanding and grow. His development had been arrested for so long that it was seemingly intractable.

The longer we are entrenched at any level, the harder it is to submit to the challenges that should lead to change and growth—but this is especially true at Level 2. Growth from Level 2 to Level 3 requires the recognition that there can actually be a "win" in not winning, that always getting one's way is not really the best thing, and that learning to coordinate one's agenda with the agendas of others can provide a satisfying outcome. This realization is the contradiction needed to unstick the Level 2 understanding. Unfortunately, it is a realization that the forty-six-year-old participant in the previous story has not been able to make. He continues to make sense of new relationships and circumstances, and even himself, through his egocentric, Level 2 lens. His consequences of not growing are a devastated ex-wife and children who will have to create a healthy environment in which to grow without the help of a higher functioning husband and father.

> Level 2 leaders are trapped by their strong and impulsive need to win. We will help them make progress if we can convince them new behaviors will still enable them to win, but with a different definition of what "winning" means. The goal is to push them to see how they are connected to others and be very clear about the consequences if they fail to improve.

Motivating Growth Toward Level 3

Creating steps that will motivate Vertical development toward Level 3 can be a little tricky. It is essential to meet people where they are, so any initial Level 3 behaviors must at first be rewarded through the person's still-Level-2 lens, which can create confusion. Behaviors that require Level 2s to suspend their own agenda and coordinate it with others' agendas need to be rewarded. When they see that coordinating agendas actually leads to a "win," it contradicts the Level 2 understanding that achieving their *own* agenda is a win.

What is a win for a Level 2 adult? Is it an "Atta boy"? Maybe not. For them, affirmation usually needs to be more tangible, like a trophy or a certificate or a perk. But remember, you're not rewarding their effort; you're rewarding the coordination of their agenda with another's.

Let me give some examples: When my child, JT, was in middle school and in the early stages of the transition between Level 2 and Level 3, he got a little bossy with a classmate I'll call Tim. Tim felt picked on by JT and told his dad, who called the principal. JT received a detention, and we grounded him at home as well. (These were negative consequences, both of which he experienced as a loss.) The principal and I also met to discuss a strategy for creating a win for JT if he would get to know Tim and make an effort to include him in the larger groups of kids (thus reinforcing the Level 3 behaviors of community and reciprocity). We asked JT to do this not only with Tim, but also with others who had been marginalized or didn't exactly fit in. JT is a popular kid, so this opportunity was in his wheel-house, and because pleasing the principal, his mom, and me mattered to JT, it could be defined as a win for him.

One night as JT was winding down for bedtime, he and I talked about what he learned about Tim—what he liked, what he was good at, and so forth. JT began to step into Tim's shoes and see things from Tim's perspective. The ability to empathize and to take responsibility for the other's well-being is a Level 3 way of understanding others. As JT got to know Tim, he began to realize that his oversimplified views of Tim were incorrect. Tim was more than "the quiet kid" who was easy to pick on. This realization, promoted by the challenge of being held accountable to incorporate Tim into the larger circle of kids, and coupled with both his principal's and parents' approval as a reward, created a contradiction to his Level 2 understanding suffi-cient enough to result in growth toward Level 3.

The effort we made with JT was essentially the same approach I took with Bob, the coaching client I mentioned earlier (although Bob was a thirty-three-year-old version). Bob had never considered the input or feelings of others from his Level 2, me-first focus. We started small. The first thing I had him do was simply ask his assistant about her plans for the upcoming Thanksgiving holiday. In the six years she had worked with him, he had never talked to her about anything but what he needed from her at work. Believe it or not, this assignment created great tension for him even though it would seem completely ordinary to anyone at Level 3 or beyond. He wasn't at all comfortable confronting his fear of losing by engaging in this kind of relational vulnerability. Yet he persevered, and his effort went surprisingly well. His assistant actually thanked him for asking, inquired as to his plans in return, and commented to others (including his boss) about how friendly he seemed all of a sudden. In debriefing the encounter with me, Bob was able to identify all of these positive "rewards" as a win for himself.

Bob's story sounds so elementary that I'm almost embarrassed to include it in this chapter, but it illustrates how strange it can feel to facilitate growth in a thirty-something-year-old that should have occurred in middle school. Bob and I built on this early success and raised the stakes over the next couple of months. He had "listening" sessions with colleagues to understand their perspectives on conflictual issues, during which he wasn't allowed to share his perspective unless asked. As a "homework assignment" he interviewed his boss to understand what the boss thought was important about company values and purpose. I instructed Bob to repeat back what he heard his boss say until the boss had nothing more to add (and I advised the boss ahead of time what to expect). Eventually Bob began to raise issues that were of concern to him only after first getting others' perspectives and confirming that they felt understood.

All of these steps helped Bob coordinate his agenda with others in a way that created notable recognition from his coworkers and boss. He recognized the wins—respect and recognition, reduction of conflict, and his own contributions being heard and valued in new ways. It was a grownup version of JT's understanding that he could win by helping others fit in. The reason Bob's story seems so odd is because we aren't used to treating thirty-year-olds like thirteen-year-olds. However, by knowing the Map, meeting others where they are, and only stretching them to the next, necessary step on their Vertical journey, we are able to accelerate growth in those whose development is arrested.

One of the biggest challenges of talent management is successfully promoting a good contributor to supervisor or manager. The very individualistic, sometimes "me-first" behaviors that make them so successful as individual contributors aren't the kinds of behaviors needed to develop and lead teams. Many organizations make the mistake of impulsively promoting the most proficient individual contributors, only to find out later the person's leader level isn't commensurate with the requirements for leading successful teams.

Level 2 leaders often see themselves as independent agents, which severely limits the possibilities for advancement since most 21st-century work demands interdependence and effective teamwork. Level 2 leaders depend too much on self-reliance to get things done. Every virtue can turn into a weakness. Thriftiness can turn into cheapness! The near enemies of self-reliance are arrogance ("I don't care what others think") and self-righteousness ("I'm better than you, and don't you forget it!"). In developing Level 2 leaders, it helps to show them how their independence, work ethic, and intelligence can make them intimidating to others, turning their strengths into weaknesses.

Where facilitating others' growth gets really tough is with severely arrested Level 2 people like Stan, the forty-three-year-old, Level 2 manager whom I described in Chapter 3. One of the very difficult things for me in choosing a career focused on facilitating the growth of others is that I don't see much hope for developing the Stans of the world. For someone to have the Vertical development of a thirteen-year-old at age forty-three, something has most likely gone terribly wrong in the past. When someone's development has been arrested for thirty years, there are usually contributing factors from their childhood. In such situations, facilitating development to a higher level usually requires psychological counseling or therapy. I am not suggesting that facilitating someone's Vertical growth in cases of severely arrested development is impossible, but anyone who attempts to do so needs to know ahead of time that the effort and costs involved will likely be significant.

Accelerating Growth from Level 2 to Level 3

Developmental growth is difficult at every level. At Level 2 where we are comfortable with a me-first way of understanding the world, the developmental disruption comes when we see that attending to only our own agenda actually limits our success. We discover that our concrete understanding leads to being ostracized from some group we want to be part of. And we are confused to realize that "getting my way" might actually result in a loss.

For most people, the shift in understanding to Level 3 takes place over a ten-year period during the teenage years, but growth can be accelerated. Even a teenager can accelerate Vertical maturity, but it won't be easy since it will require giving up one's Level 2 outlook. In fact, accelerated Vertical growth usually won't happen without some help from parents or other trusted authorities. It takes great discipline for a parent to enforce Level 2 consequences on one hand while at the same time promoting more adult (Level 3) concepts of reciprocity and openness to the influence of others. It requires that parents think about what they need to do in advance, get out of reactive mode, and become intentional about the growth of their children.

This is much more doable if parents are Level 4 dominant, or fast approaching it. It also helps if they understand Level 3 behavior in order to model and promote it. Parents still at Level 3 are trying to understand and self-author what *they* want to be about, what *they* stand for, and the values that *they* hold, so they aren't really ready to help someone else get there. For another thing, only at Level 4 are we able to stop being defined by the performance of others—especially our children. We must become *less connected* to their performance even as we help create an understanding of their *connectedness* to the family system and the world at large.

In my experience, Level 2 people in their twenties are better able to accelerate their growth than teenagers. With twenty-somethings, it is as though a pent-up demand for growth is waiting to be unleashed, so growth can be accelerated through sharing the Map for development, pointing out the consequences of their Level 2 behaviors, and helping them make sense of a new Level 3 way of understanding the world, self, and others. However, even though Level 2 twenty-somethings may be more *ready* to grow toward Level 3 than teenagers, they will still be reluctant to let go of the Level 2 stability they have established and grown comfortable with during the last ten to fifteen years.

They will also continue to make sense of everything from the outside in as they grow toward and into Level 3, so their hand must be held through this transition—we must become the outside source they will need to make sense of this new way of understanding. We will need to help them define appropriate Level 3 responses. We will have to help them understand others' perspectives. We will have to help them see how suspending their own agenda can actually increase their success. In short, we will have to help them let go of their Level 2 perspective and start to see through a Level 3 lens.

Level 4 leaders need to understand that words may have different meanings when used by their Level 2 employees. A vocabulary that makes perfect sense at Level 4 can dumb-found those at Level 2. When communicating with those at different levels, learn to clarify what others are saying . . . and never be too quick to assume they understand what *you're* saying.

While it is often possible to accelerate growth from Level 2 to Level 3, there are exceptions. Sometimes a person's childhood experiences, especially home life, are so destructive that his or her development is locked in at Level 2. Such situations often involve some sort of abuse at the hands of a Level 2 authority—a parent or other adult—requiring that the victim get professional psychological counseling to sort through those experiences, break the grip of their Level 2 understanding, and start to grow. We can sympathize greatly with the unfairness of the situation. We can empathize with the person's need to self-protect in order to function. But such people need more help and therapy than even a business psychologist is equipped to provide. Our most compassionate response is to encourage them to work with a good counselor so that they can experience the joy of continuing to grow.

You might find yourself in a relationship with someone (late thirties or beyond) whose development has been arrested at Level 2 for so long that facilitating growth seems futile. The question then becomes, do you have the influence or capacity to motivate the person to change? If he or she won't get help and you have no ability to create consequences, then your best option might be to exit the relationship in order to protect your own ability to continue growing. For someone who feels unsafe in a romantic or marriage relationship, suspending the relationship is necessary until healing and growth can occur. Don't be misled into believing the other person will change before being forced to deal with consequences that challenge his or her Level 2 understanding. I know this sounds harsh, but the destructive wake that follows Level 2 adults can easily devastate you if you don't objectively evaluate your ability to facilitate growth in them.

Stress and Growth

Karl noted earlier that we are often asked if people can be at different levels of development in different situations or environments. Not really, because your current lens is your current lens and it doesn't change in different circumstances or situations. However, development is not neat and linear, so it might *appear* as if someone is Level 2 in some places and Level 3 at others. Additionally, when we are in transition from one level to the next, we progress much better when we are not under stress. When we start feeling stressed out, we tend to revert to what we know for sure—our previous level. At every level of development, progress is a matter of "two steps forward, one step back," but it is perhaps most obvious during the transition from Level 2 to Level 3.

When my oldest child, Alex, was in high school, we would sometimes see her engage in fully Level 3 kinds of conversations with adults—our friends or the parents of her friends. She showed understanding and compassion, and we were proud that she seemed

so grown up! But if those adults left and we told her we were having dinner together as a family on a night she had hoped to be with
her friends, it created stress for her. In the blink of an eye, she would
revert from such surprising maturity to being a me-first, Level 2 teenager again. The transformation was a sight to behold.

Even though Alex had experienced the rewards of acting like a
contributing member of a larger family and community—receiving
praise, less tension, smiles and laughter—under stress she was unable
to maintain her newly developing Level 3 understanding, and she
immediately defaulted to manipulating circumstances to achieve her
agenda. Some of her manipulations included screaming, resisting,
crying, and ultimately sulking her way through the meal, hoping we
wouldn't again have the nerve to pull a stunt like asking her to have
dinner with the family on the wrong night again!

We knew she was completely capable of handling this circumstance like a Level 3 young adult. We had seen her do it many times.
At her best she could share what was important to her, what she
had planned for the evening, and even what was important to us.
She could empathize with our position and attempt to coordinate
her agenda with ours by seeking a compromise to meet our desire
for family time. The irony is that she was more likely to "win" when
she acted like she didn't need to. We might reward the more mature
approach by granting her request when she acted Level 3, but were
much more likely to hold firm and enforce consequences when she
took a Level 2 approach.

When we're feeling stressed out, our normal ways of dealing
with and understanding our world are not working. If they were, we
wouldn't feel stressed out, would we? During growth transitions from

one level to the next we are attempting to discover the "new normal" at the *next* level—in Alex's case, Level 3. But if we feel like this new level is not working, or is not going to work, what we usually try is what we know for sure—the level of development where we have spent the last several years. On a positive note, just recognizing this phenomenon in ourselves is an indication of developmental progress. Acknowledging it also accelerates development to the next level because we are much more capable of dealing with something we name for what it is.

In fact, our biggest opportunities to accelerate growth may be during particularly stressful situations. The challenge seems bigger and the contradiction to our current level greater when the pressure is on. As we try to facilitate the development of people (children or adults) from Level 2 to Level 3, we can leverage these "stress" opportunities for even greater growth . . . if we are able to keep our wits about us. This effort requires more energy and intentionality than efforts made during calmer times. If we get sucked into arguments, lose our cool, or are just too tired to deal with the person, we will miss the opportunity. But disciplining ourselves to make this purposeful investment will not only pay forward the growth of the other, but will also reduce the amount of energy we will need later if we don't make the investment. Seize challenges in real time to really accelerate growth.

This past year my teenage daughter signed up to volunteer at a local food bank on a Saturday. Two days before the event, her tennis coach asked to her play a match that

Saturday morning. My daughter asked me, "What should I do?"

I had a good idea what she should do, but I told her, "It's your decision. Think about it and do what you think is best. I'll support you either way." Her immediate response was what you would expect from a fifteen-year-old: "But Dad, that's not fair!"

Later that evening she came back and said, "Someone is going to be let down. I want to play tennis, but I committed to the food bank first."

I was pleased she chose working at the food bank. And she was right about someone feeling let down by her choice. I am sure the tennis coach and the team were less than pleased with her decision.

She didn't enjoy making that hard choice, but it was her decision to make. I could have told her what to do, but I would have robbed her of the opportunity to struggle and think through her decision.

For most adults, the transition out of Level 2 is a thing of the past. We are able to put our desire to win in perspective, and it no longer defines us. We understand the simplicity and certainty of concrete facts, but can still subjugate them to the hypothetical or what is possible. We are able to *have* an agenda without *being* that agenda.

Accelerating the growth of others to Level 3 is a matter of identifying and accepting the nature of the Level 2 mindset, realizing the person is only ready and able to move a step at a time toward the next level. Look for opportunities to become one of the outside sources to help the Level 2 people you know make sense of the world in a new, better, Level 3 way.

Consider This . . .

1. Think back to your childhood. What *childish* Level 2 behaviors can you recall? Do you still struggle with any of them?

2. When your own Level 2 perspective on life became too limiting and you needed to continue with your Vertical growth, in what ways (if any) did your parents help you (e.g., rewards and punishments, allowing you to suffer consequences of actions, etc.)?

3. What behaviors have you noticed in your own children (or those of close friends or relatives) that you would classify as Level 2? What could you do (or did you do) to help them get beyond their me-first perspective and move on toward Level 3?

4. How about adults you know? Does anyone appear to be stalled at Level 2? If so, do you feel there is still hope for the person, or is it too late for him or her to change? What do you think is the best course of action at this point?

5. Can you recall a time when a stressful situation affected your own developmental growth? If so, what did you learn from the experience?

Chapter 10

FROM LEVEL 3 TO LEVEL 4: OWNING YOUR PERSPECTIVE

I have told plenty of stories on my kids throughout this book, so it is only fair that I tell one on myself at this point. When I was about fifteen, I became best friends with a guy named Mark—the one who made the journey to California with me. At the time I was completely susceptible to peer pressure and would follow the lead of most any crowd I was in. My parents were good about creating consequences when I hung out with "the wrong crowd," and they encouraged my association with kids who were making wise decisions. Mark was one of the good kids, and my parents gave me great freedom to do all sorts of things as long as I did them with Mark. I was a Mark clone, totally defined by his understanding of the world.

But when Mark and I finished high school, we went to different colleges. I joined a fraternity a couple of weeks before classes started, and all of a sudden I had a new set of outside sources to help shape my view of the world. Unfortunately the influence of this group, combined with my highly extroverted personality and completely Level 3 Vertical maturity, was a wicked combination. I got sucked into the party scene and wanted to be a part of any group that was going to do anything social—which, as it turned out, was some group almost every night. This scenario didn't mix well with the primary reason I was in college, and my grades reflected my inability to handle the tension between learning and living.

The evening before spring break of my freshman year I had partied like a rock star with some guys from the fraternity. Green and queasy from the night before, I crawled into the passenger seat of my roommate's non-air-conditioned 1974 Capri sedan, prepared to endure the six-hour drive to visit a buddy in Florida. Trey looked over and asked me, "So how's this working out for you?"

The answer was that life hadn't been working out for quite some time, and it *especially* wasn't working out that morning. The challenges of the relationships and circumstances that had been defining me had created an unavoidable contradiction. I could clearly see the chinks in the armor of continuing on a path determined by others, and I realized that the outcomes of staying on that path were becoming increasingly unacceptable. At that moment I began moving from Level 3.0 to 3.2. I was now able to see that being defined by this group wasn't what I wanted for my life.

When people see the weakness in their own way of thinking, they realize that what may have worked so well (perhaps for many years) starts to break down, and they experience failure. In Keith's case, keeping the approval of his friends by doing the things they wanted to do came at an increasingly high cost. Feeling "green" in a too-hot Capri for six hours was a breaking point for Keith—a realization that he wanted to live a different way. It was a wakeup call. Mine came as a sophomore at Penn State, at the time too defined by my role as a football player. While lying in a hospital suffering from a total separation of my shoulder and pleading to the nurse for more morphine, I knew I needed a new direction for my life. I was at a crossroads, although I had no idea at the time what that meant.

When Trey and I returned from spring break, I resolved to get my life together and set a new course. The decision was my first glimpse of self-authorship. It is what defines being 3.2, but because it was *only* 3.2, I intuitively knew that I still needed the help of some outside source—and I definitely wanted a *different* outside source that would help me make sense of the world in a way consistent with this new "partially owned" vision of who I wanted to become.

I grabbed the yellow pages (which, for you younger readers not up on your ancient history, was the closest thing we had to Google in 1981) and found a nearby local church. It had to be close enough for bike travel, since I didn't have a car. In this new environment, I began to meet the kind of men I had determined I wanted to be. They invested in me as mentors and became the outside sources I needed to help me make sense of myself, others, and circumstances in a way that was consistent with my newly forming personal goals. These men helped put my life on a new course and it sustained me through much of my early twenties. However, as I entered my mid-twenties, various challenges that contradicted the input of these mentors began to move me from 3.2 to 3.4. In other words, I began to take ownership of more of my own understanding even as I continued to seek mentors as outside sources that were consistent with the new me I was becoming.

Additionally, and because the outside sources with which I affiliated had a faith component, the ideology of the church became a big influence in shaping my understanding, as did my parents, my girlfriend (soon to be wife), her parents, and, as I moved into my twenties, the influences of the organizations I worked for. It was a constant back-and-forth growth cycle between being shaped by these outside sources, challenged by experiences and circumstances that didn't fit neatly into this evolving understanding, and increasingly deciding what I believed from the inside out.

This dynamic continued into my early thirties as I grew from 3.2 to 3.4. My effectiveness as a leader became greater as I gained Inside-Out clarity about who and what I wanted to be. When I was thirty I decided to return to school and pursue a doctorate in psychology, which set me on the career path that I have practiced for the last twenty-plus years. Graduate school was a great source of influence and refinement during what I know now were my 3.4 to 3.6 years. While graduate school was a significant outside influence in shaping my understanding, it also became the source of my greatest challenge.

By the time I started graduate school, I was beginning to be very self-authored in many areas of my life. I knew I wanted to help people become all they were meant to be and that graduate school would refine my ability to do that. I had a clear sense of who I wanted to be as a husband and father, even as I welcomed mentors to help me shape and refine that understanding. I felt very solid in my faith and was drawing conclusions through the iterative process of challenges intersecting with my current understanding as well as the input of outside sources (church, authors, and mentors), and authoring my own understanding.

However, faith was the very issue that created the biggest challenge I would face in my transition from Level 3 to Level 4. It was my midlife transition because pursuing my Ph.D. rocked the foundations of the faith that held together so much of how I understood myself, others, and the world. Even though my course of study was focused on the psychology of business, the *challenges* of being confronted with the philosophies of knowledge, reality, and existence created such a significant *contradiction* to the understanding of my faith that I felt like a rug had been pulled out from under me.

> When one outside source ceases to be effective, someone at Level 3 often tries to replace it with another outside source, when the real goal is to become more Inside-Out.

Because I wasn't willing to simply adopt every perspective of all my professors (a new set of outside sources), the next several years were an intellectual and emotional journey that required me to let go of how I understood the world, myself, and others. I was challenged to gain a new understanding: my gateway to an Inside-Out, Level 4 understanding.

Letting go wasn't easy. Actually, it's the most difficult challenge I've encountered in my life. It was the very intensity of the challenge, and the resulting contradiction, that created such a momentous opportunity for accelerated growth. But in order to realize that opportunity, I had to let go of the stability of what I knew and undergo the painstaking process of figuring out for myself where I was going to come down on the fundamental questions of life, faith, existence, and everything. My wife, reflecting back on that time, says (quite tongue-in-cheek, and pun intended) that those years scared the hell out of her.

My influence in helping others walk through their transitions these days has much more depth and nuance than when I began and had a more provincial, Outside-In understanding. My understanding at Level 3.6 seemed adequate, but it didn't have the depth it has now because I didn't fully own it. I hadn't dealt with the challenges that came through submitting myself to the study of philosophy.

I'm not trying to create a memoir here, but the full story is a book in itself. We can discuss it over coffee sometime, but suffice it to say the basic tenets of my faith didn't ultimately change. Rather, they became more real and complete because they became mine from the inside out.

The transformation during those years was scary, confusing, destabilizing, and emotional. That said, I still wouldn't avoid that challenge if I could to go back in time and do it all over again. Being able to gain a perspective on not only the influences that support my conclusions but also those that contradict my beliefs has made me more effective in leading others and myself on the journey of continued growth.

If you come from a different faith perspective or have drawn different conclusions, I get that. I'm simply telling my story because it is my experience and illustrates well what it means and feels like to go from Level 3 to Level 4. My hope is that you can make connections in your own journey if you are between these two levels—connections between the difficulties of letting go of an old way of understanding to gain an even better, self-authored understanding. It won't be easy, but you will become much more effective when you are able to objectively incorporate the pros and cons of positions and beliefs that both counter and support your ultimate self-authored conclusions.

Most of our professional clients are at the transition between Level 3 and Level 4. The shift to a full Level 4 understanding of yourself and others is a significant challenge. Like all major transitions, this one involves loss. When we're in our 20s, most of us want to party with our friends. In our 30s, being a part of a meaningful social network is important, and in our 40s, most of us are trying to add value to our companies and institutions. Relinquishing those identities (and the accrued benefits) is terribly hard to do. In fact, some never make the transition. Some find so much comfort in their social standing that they never acknowledge the limits, costs, and risks associated with that limiting definition of identity. Security wins out. Keith's word for the transition to Level 4 is "scary," which is the best word to describe every transition to another level because of the losses perceived or imagined.

Developmental Challenges from Level 3 to Level 4

At pure Level 3 (3.0) we are fully defined by outside sources. As we involve ourselves with personal relationships, organizations, and ideologies, we readily adopt others' views. In the move from Level 3 to Level 4, the same three principles of growth apply that were listed in the previous chapter: (1) Challenges need to intersect with our current lens in a way that contradicts our understanding; (2) The benefits of growing need to outweigh the discomfort of remaining where we are; and (3) We need to let go to grow. But even though these three principles remain the same, the Vertical transformation from Level 3 to Level 4 will look different than it looked from Level 2 to Level 3 or will look from Level 4 to Level 5.

The more Level 3 dominant we are, the more we will feel outstripped by the demands of situations that cannot be resolved using previously learned solutions. Robert Kegan titled one of his books on this subject *In Over Our Heads: The Mental Demands of Modern Life*.[40] The title paints the picture. If challenging situations could be understood by applying previously learned, Outside-In solutions, they wouldn't contradict our current understanding and we wouldn't feel in over our heads. It is only because they unsettle us that they are instrumental to development.

The challenges that lead to growth in the transition from Level 3 to Level 4 come in three basic forms: circumstantial challenges, relational challenges, and belief challenges.

Circumstantial Challenges

Circumstantial challenges intersect our Level 3 understanding when we find ourselves faced with situations in which we don't know what to do (or when we are investing in the development of someone else in a similar situation). We are not handling our circumstances; they are handling us. Our current lens lacks the capacity to see the situation clearly. It is like we have put on someone else's eyeglasses and our vision (our understanding of what we need to do) is blurry. We are at a loss for how to handle what needs to be done.

Some circumstantial challenges are often not only difficult, but also negative. The death of a loved one, the loss of a job, or extended financial difficulty can all intersect with a Level 3 lens in a way that makes it unclear what to do next. Yet such unavoidable situations provide an opportunity for Vertical growth. At Level 3 we need to seize these challenges and do the difficult work of determining a new Inside-Out way of making sense of the circumstances. If we ignore them, run away from them, or cover them up with alcohol, distractions, faith, or exercise (which might not be bad things in and of themselves), an ideal growth opportunity is lost.

Other circumstances are entirely positive, yet they can be just as challenging and difficult to perceive clearly with a Level 3 understanding. Getting married, having children, or receiving a job promotion are all opportunities for significant growth. They are ideal times to seize the challenge to gain a clearer understanding of who we should be and how we should respond. We lose the opportunity if we continue to be defined by an Outside-In understanding and force new and contradictory circumstances through the lens of outside sources rather than our own.

For most people who develop at a normal pace, growth-oriented responses to circumstantial challenges happen naturally over time. However—and this point is big—when we are familiar with the Map, we are able to recognize the Level 3 lens for what it is and know there's a new and better Inside-Out perspective on the world and ourselves. If we decide to let our circumstantial challenges be catalysts for change, we can accelerate our Vertical growth to Level 4—a greater degree of effectiveness and satisfaction.

Relational Challenges

At Level 3 we are defined by the relationships we have, so it makes sense that relational challenges will be significant in the transition from Level 3 to 4. Loosely speaking, a relationship can also include a role, a group, or even an institution that defines us, but for the time being let's focus on personal relationships. As we become Level 3, we allow our relationships to determine our understanding and well-being. When everything is going well in the relationship, we are doing well. However, any difficulty in a relationship challenges our understanding.

A lot of blaming takes place at Level 3, so any close relationship—especially a romantic one—will experience some tension. We say things like, "You made me feel lousy," or "He made me angry," or "She's making this so hard." Yet if we see that the challenge is intersecting with our inadequate Level 3, Outside-In understanding and choose to lean into it, the relational challenge provides an opportunity for growth.

This phenomenon permeated my growth story that opened this chapter. I could see that my fraternity was certainly contributing to the destructive decisions I was making, but it was the tension of realizing negative consequences associated with those decisions that created the opportunity to take more ownership and begin to grow.

When I got married, my beautiful wife and I were both Level 3 dominant, and I can assure you I created a lot of growth opportunities for her. My most memorable growth opportunities came when I felt my relationships with my philosophy professors were undermining my faith. I held them responsible because I didn't have an understanding of the Map at that time. In retrospect, it could have been my cue to recognize the growth challenges they were providing.

The point is that relational challenges intersect our Level 3 lens with a purpose. They prompt us to grow by forcing us to ask, "Who do I want to be?" or "What's the story I want to tell?" When we start to ask those questions, we give ourselves the opportunity to accelerate development. Any time we find ourselves blaming someone or something else, it's a cue that a challenge is intersecting with the comfort of our Level 3 lens, and the opportunity to grow is right in front of us.

Belief Challenges

The final broad category to consider is challenges to what we hold to be true. I used an example of a challenge to my faith, but that is just one aspect of a belief challenge. More broadly, beliefs are what we hold to be true about the way the world works, and that may or may not include one's faith.

We live in a unique time. Technological advances have opened up an entire world unavailable to previous generations. We have almost instantaneous exposure to people and cultures all over the world via streaming video. Images and perspectives from cultures completely foreign to ours are available to anyone with a TV or an Internet connection. One result for many of us is that what we hold to be true is challenged constantly. Some respond to this challenge by surrounding themselves with like-minded people and perspectives. But a better option is to pursue real growth by beginning to self-author our own perspectives in a way that incorporates some of the different perspectives. Doing this alone can be difficult, but intentionally engaging with others in developmental relationships can rapidly accelerate growth.

As I stated earlier, most of our clients come to us in the transition between Levels 3 and 4. At that pivotal point in their lives and careers, they feel the organization's expectations of them to be an Inside-Out leader—a Level 4 perspective—but they feel the demands are outstripping their capacity to understand and adapt. Every time leaders feel this awkward sensation, they have bumped into a potential opportunity for growth.

Don't miss your opportunity!

Motivating Growth Toward Level 4

At Level 2, growth is motivated by tangible, external wins or losses. In contrast, at Level 3, growth is driven more by discomfort when outside-sourced understanding comes in tension with contradictory circumstances or information. Removal of the discomfort can be accomplished in one of two ways. One option is to force it through our current lens without changing our understanding, resulting in no growth. The far better option is to lean into the tension and grow. The Inside-Out resolution of this tension is its own reward.

What feels most natural and comfortable at Level 3 is to work our hardest to resolve conflicts "so we can all just get along." Valuing agreement in our relationships is not a bad yearning, yet this "solve it" response tends to arrest development. A growth response assumes more personal responsibility by determining what we stand for, understanding others' positions in a way that they feel heard, without feeling the need to agree and taking ownership of a new understanding of oneself and the other in the midst of the differences that led to the conflict. This growth-oriented approach doesn't make the quality of the relationship contingent upon agreeing with one another, which can be very freeing. It allows us to become who we are meant to be even as it allows others to do the same. Increasingly experiencing this Inside-Out feeling motivates continued growth to Level 4.

Circumstantial challenges can also motivate growth. A good example is the challenge of financial difficulty. When money gets tight, the contradictions provided by the challenge (evaluating and prioritizing spending, aligning expenditures with values, resolving the tension between earning money and spending time with the family, etc.) prompt a reevaluation of who we want to be and the story we want to tell. A bit of a struggle at that point provides the necessary ingredients for growth. But if we are able to easily obtain money to fix the challenge before it does its work, we don't grow.

This dynamic helps explain why multigenerational family wealth often results in noticeable developmental immaturity in the third generation. It takes a great deal of intentionality, first by parents, then by the young adult children, to resist the easy road of buying away challenges with cars, credit cards, vacations, and the like. It is possible to grow in the midst of financial ease, but it is more difficult to identify and seize growth challenges when we have the capacity to minimize or remove them with financial resources.

At any period of relative ease we tend to grow at a slower rate. When everything is going well at work and with the family, we don't face as many challenges that have the potential to contradict our understanding. I'm not saying that you should shy away from success, but I am suggesting that during times of abundance we need to be more intentional about submitting to and seizing the more subtle opportunities for growth.

I'll say it again: the Inside-Out reconciliation of the contradiction provided by challenges, whether unavoidable or intentional, is its own reward. Gaining an Inside-Out, self-authored understanding is not only a more effective way to live and work; it feels better to boot!

Accelerating Growth from Level 3 to Level 4

Accelerating growth from Level 3 to Level 4 is achieved by constantly asking yourself questions demanding self-authored answers. You would do well to post such questions on your bathroom mirror during the transition:

Who do I want to be?

What is the story I want to tell?

What matters most to me?

What am I willing to stand for?

How will I know what to do?

These questions apply whether we're facing uninvited challenges or intentionally identifying points of tension that can become gateways for growth. The same set of questions that accelerate your own growth during this transition can also benefit others in whose development you are investing.

As you ponder these questions over a period of time, you should begin to see opportunities for growth that are as clear as if they were highlighted with a neon arrow pointing to a flashing sign reading "Use me! Use me!" Your complaints are perhaps the most obvious opportunities, as you saw in Chapter 8. But other signs include blaming others, sleepless nights, relational dilemmas, and the like.

I realize I may sound a little repetitive by this point, but please bear with me. In every Level 3 coaching relationship, when my clients hear themselves spontaneously complaining or blaming, they will actually beat me to the punch and say, "I know, I know—a new opportunity for growth. Give it a rest!" But when the truth soaks in and they recognize the value of their complaints and/or blaming as a tool to help them identify challenges and take responsibility for their own development, they can take the first step to accelerating their growth to a place of greater effectiveness and satisfaction.

If you are investing in the growth of people at Level 3, you also need to patiently and repetitively attempt to keep them on course. At that level they still need an outside source, and you might be just the one to help them get on a growth track. You can ask them the questions that lead to Inside-Out, Level 4 answers. Because they are Outside-In, you might need to prompt them with an answer now and then, but don't be too quick to make a habit of it. Of course it would be easier to just answer the questions for them. Ask any parent or boss: it takes less time in the short run to just tell a Level 3 follower what to do than it does to steer the person through the developmental process. However, in the long run the more effective option is investing in their development—something like the difference between handing someone a fish and teaching him to fish.

If you're a Level 4 leader, take the time to explain to others the way you're leading them. Be intentional in developing others by explaining what you're doing and why. If your leadership style revolves around a strong value you have, name it, and explain why you're using it. If accountability or responsibility is important to you, don't be afraid to use it frequently and define it for your team.

By holding yourself up to a higher standard, you set a standard for others. We all trip and stumble on occasion—and sometimes we have to admit we're wrong—but clear goals and standards let others know what we stand for, and just as importantly, what we expect from them.

The transition from Level 3 to Level 4 takes great courage. It demands we let go of the support system that has worked for us for quite some time. It requires that we lessen our reliance on those who have helped us define and make sense of our worlds—including spouses and children. It means we must let go of the ideologies that have shaped our belief system—even a faith ideology to which we may have intense emotional and spiritual attachment. And it demands a great level of trust that when we let go we aren't going to fall into the abyss.

"There is a time in every man's education when he arrives at the conviction that envy is ignorance; that imitation is suicide; that he must take himself for better, for worse, as his

> portion; that though the wide universe is full of good, no kernel of nourishing corn can come to him but through his toil bestowed on that plot of ground which is given him to till. The power which resides in him is new in nature, and none but he knows what that is which he can do, nor does he know until he has tried."
>
> —Ralph Waldo Emerson, "Self-Reliance"

Unavoidable challenges can be a gift, even though they may be the hardest things we ever experience. Losing a parent, child, spouse, or dear friend is nothing we would ever sign up for, yet most anyone who has been through such a difficulty often reflects back on that time as one leading to great growth.

It is my hope for those in the transition between Levels 3 and 4 that the insights gained in this chapter will give both courage and traction to navigate this segment of the developmental journey in a new way. I encourage you to not do it alone. Remember that we all grow faster when we are in developmentally focused relationships with other people. When we are vulnerable and transparent with those we can trust, our developmental challenges open the door to growth, which results in a greater level of satisfaction, happiness, peace, and well-being—from the inside out.

Consider This . . .

1. What would you say is the most difficult challenge you have undergone so far? What did you learn from that experience?

2. List some challenges you have recently faced (or are currently facing) in each of these categories. Then, for each one, determine whether you are trying to avoid it, cover it up, or lean into it.

    Circumstantial Challenges?

    Relational Challenges?

    Belief Challenges?

3. If you are not yet at Level 4, has this chapter made you want to get there? Why or why not? What is the next step you would need to take?

4. Do you know someone at Level 3 whom you would like to help grow? If so, how might you accelerate his or her growth based on specific circumstances the person is facing?

Chapter 11

FROM LEVEL 4 TO LEVEL 5: FINDING FIFTH GEAR

I opened this book by asking you to consider your Promised Land. What are the hopes and dreams that are tucked away in the deepest recesses of your heart? What are you hoping to accomplish with your life? What kind of person do you truly want to be?

We have said that almost anyone is capable of getting to Level 5 and experiencing life at a deeper level than ever before. But we have also said that fewer than fifteen percent of the population ever gets there. What's the problem? Why don't more of us ever taste the milk and honey?

Progress is never easy. If we go back to the original quest for the Promised Land—the Exodus of the Hebrew people from Egypt to Israel—it's not a pretty story. It was no simple matter to break free after being enslaved for more than 400 years. When they finally did, Moses gave a powerful demonstration at the Red Sea of how a difficult challenge could really be a growth opportunity, but the lesson didn't stick. Every subsequent challenge the people faced was a source of grumbling and dissension. When they finally got to the brink of their destination, twelve scouts were sent ahead to explore the territory. They saw the fruit of the Promised Land (including a single cluster of grapes so massive it took two men to carry it on a pole between them), but when they returned, ten of them warned of giants in the land—which sent the people into a panic. More than once on the journey, they had proposed *going back to the slavery of Egypt* rather than dealing with the new challenge and opportunity. This time they even plotted to stone those who would impede their efforts to make the return trip to Egypt with a new leader (see Numbers 14:1–10).

Getting all the way to the Promised Land is difficult. Really difficult. The Israelites grew to detest desert life so much they just wanted out—even if that meant going back into slavery. As we have seen, stressful situations can make us want to retreat to a familiar place. However, these days more people are probably stalled due to the *ease* of life rather than difficulty, so today's leaders may tend to relate more to Odysseus than Moses when it comes to trying to motivate people to keep growing.

Odysseus's Promised Land was Ithaca. After the Trojan War, all he wanted to do was get home, but he was confronted with one crisis after another. Some of his biggest obstacles were the alluring pleasantries he encountered. He learned ahead of time of (and managed to avoid) the threat of the Sirens who would lure sailors to shipwreck with their irresistible songs. But when he found himself in the Land of the Lotus Eaters, his men never came back from scouting the island because life there (primarily due to the intoxicating lotus fruit) was so good they had no desire to ever go anywhere else. Odysseus had to track them down, drag them back to the ship, and lock them up so he could continue his journey.

Whenever we get to a place that is pretty good, it just seems the essence of wisdom to not make waves at that point. We stick with what works, and ignorance can be bliss for a long, long time—even when the Map promises an even better destination just a little farther ahead.

For many people, Level 4 is a siren song. After finally making that difficult transition from Outside-In thinking to an Inside-Out understanding of the world and the ability to make decisions without fearing what others might think, life becomes *so* much better. Truth be told, at that level you've learned enough to manage the rest of your life reasonably well . . . and many people do just that. Level 4 is a welcome milepost along the way, but it is still just an oasis. You're not all the way through the desert yet.

That's why the most difficult growth challenge is from Level 4 to Level 5. The difficulty has to do with what we must give up to gain something new and better. Between Level 1 and Level 2 we give up our perceptions as reality to gain a more concrete understanding. From Level 2 to Level 3 we give up simplistic certainty and winning to gain connectedness with others. Between Level 3 and Level 4 we give up our reliance on formative relationships and influences to bring a deeper, more authentic, more effective self to our relationships. But what is demanded to grow from Level 4 to Level 5 is letting go of a hard-earned, self-authored understanding of self and world in order to gain the openness that leads to greater wisdom. Giving up the Level 4 self feels like a death of the things that we are most protective of, and it feels like we are exposing ourselves to a potentially unsafe vulnerability.

Still, I don't believe people are meant to settle for less than Level 5. If we were, we wouldn't be so impressed when we encounter Level 5 sages and their rare wisdom, or aspire to be like them as we continue to grow older. After seeing what is possible, why ever settle for being a cranky, or even benign, old person arrested at Level 4?

In the move from Level 4 to Level 5, the same three principles of growth apply: challenges must intersect with our current lens in a way that contradicts our understanding; the benefits of growing (motivation) need to outweigh the discomfort of remaining where we are; and we need to let go to grow. However, the principles of accelerating development in the Vertical transformation from Level 4 to Level 5 will look different, just as it looked different between Level 2 and Level 3 and between Level 3 and Level 4.

> We all tend to look at what's in our hands to solve problems. Unless we're forced to try something new, we don't even think about other options. But suppose you're gifted at shoveling and someone asks for your advice on the best way to cross a river. It's highly unlikely you will find an option where your shovel will ever be the most efficient way to get there.
>
> Someone else might recommend building a bridge or finding a boat, at which point a wise person would learn new skills of bridge building or boat rowing. The most difficult challenge for Level 4 leaders is looking beyond their shovel. They need not throw away the shovel, because it has worked very well for many years on many different problems. The challenge is to be open to new ways of doing things, new tools, new processes, and new people.

Your way of seeing the world at Level 4 was developed in response to earlier challenges, and you are necessarily convinced it must be the most effective understanding or else you wouldn't have settled on it in the first place. This hard won Level 4-ness has been locked in by your own personal experience, so in order for new challenges to contradict this understanding enough so that you may be willing to let it go, those challenges had better be very compelling!

Some of the same unavoidable traumatic events of life that prompted the move to Level 4 can also lead on to Level 5. Losing a child or spouse (either through death or broken relationship), significant personal sickness or distress, and so forth can unsettle the self-authored world we have created. Even though comparable events may have led to the creation of our Level 4 understanding, challenging circumstances still remain the fuel for growth to Level 5. The difficulty is that from Level 4 we have never been more capable of handling challenges. We all have known people who experienced great challenges and proceeded to double down on their Level 4 understanding rather than using them to grow to the next level. Those are the times we must lose ourselves to gain ourselves—to open ourselves up to a different, potentially broader understanding. The Level 5 sage has learned to incorporate the complexity raised by the new challenge into a more comprehensive whole.

If we choose, we can make progress toward Level 5 by *intentionally* submitting ourselves to challenges that contradict our current understanding, such as exposure to other political ideologies or religious beliefs. At Level 4 we construct a narrative we tell ourselves that not only makes sense of the world around us but also explains our personal weaknesses and keeps them from being exposed. We are not good at being transparent about our vulnerabilities with others (or even with ourselves). Stated differently, we don't know what we don't know about ourselves. However, understanding these vulnerabilities as the chinks in our Level 4 armor is the first developmental movement from Level 4 to Level 5. It is growing to Level 4.2.

Voluntary Challenges

None of us want to volunteer for the traumas that offer the best opportunities to grow to Level 5, so let me suggest three challenges you can intentionally submit to as effective gateways for Level 5 growth. Each of these challenges involves people or situations close to your heart, so they provide the best connections to an inner vulnerability that you may not even be aware of. These three areas of challenge involve your family, your faith, and your biases.

I'm not assuming that everyone is married or has children, nor do I presume that you have an unhealthy understanding of people from different cultures, but we all have families and unrealized biases. I *am* assuming everyone has faith in a general sense, though not all of it is traditional. Even atheists have faith in their own logic and understanding, and such faith, like that of a deist, is held in the deepest part of who they are. Like family and bias, faith provides a potential gateway for the difficult growth to Level 5.

Family

For most of us, family provides the deepest connection to our innermost, emotional self—our heart. No one is more capable of hurting us than those who are closest to us. On the other hand, those are the most likely people to break through the barriers our Level 4 selves have constructed to ensure harmony, strength, and under-standing. We are largely unaware of our protective barriers at Level 4. In fact, the ability to take an objective view of the role that they play in helping us maintain our understanding of ourselves and others is a measure of growth toward Level 5.

Awareness of our protective barriers increases when those clos-est to us, often spouses and children, do or say things that bump up against them, making us want to respond by either lashing out or shutting down—what psychologists call "fight or flight." A comment or action contradicts something we truly desire or assume about our-selves, and the kneejerk response is to protect ourselves by fighting back or running away. Either option may "fix" the challenge by mak-ing it go away, but both will short-circuit Vertical development.

Many Level 4 people deny that their spouses or children have that degree of influence. They would say the relationship has matured to a point where conflict or hurt rarely creates a fight-or-flight response: "We have a great marriage;" "My relationship with my kids is very open and supportive;" "We never really have conflict anymore." This presumption of ongoing harmony in our closest relationships is more likely a sign of being fixed at Level 4 than a sign of mature relational perfection. Level 5 people actually are more aware of potential areas where they can improve their relationships, of how to challenge their kids' understanding, and of how conflict is an opportunity to be embraced for growth. The fact we may not often be hurt or exposed by those closest to us usually has more to do with self-protection than objectivity.

I have seen many Level 4 marriages or parent-child relationships that would be characterized as loving and secure—and they are (just as they were at Level 3, thirty years prior). But there are often minor "assaults"—a comment, a look, sarcasm, something said under the breath, or an aside to a friend. The assault is not a serious threat to the love or commitment in the relationship; rather, it is merely a response to living in a close relationship between two imperfect people. Yet rather than acknowledge it, the offended party quite often does not respond, acts like it is no big deal, laughs it off, or even gives it back in a good-natured way. One great couple I know described it as their "shtick." Self-authoring a protective mechanism to reconcile the response, even when it comes off as patient or loving, arrests growth because it has the effect of maintaining the security and understanding of one's current lens.

Intentional growth toward Level 5 comes in learning to lean into the jabs (or at least some of them) in order to gain a new and deeper understanding of our own vulnerability or weakness. I know submitting to this sounds like punishment, but challenges that contradict our current understanding are what lead to growth, and finding intentional opportunities to fuel growth is most difficult from the security and stability of Level 4. However, when we pause and try to identify the previously ignored or reconciled little twinge of pain or uncomfortable reaction we have to the jab, we potentially gain a new understanding of our own vulnerability. We realize how much we don't want to be disconnected, dismissed, rejected, invalidated, or criticized. What we really want is to be intimately connected, accepted, cheered for, loved, and supported. Admitting that from Level 4 feels weak because it contradicts the independence and strength of the self-authored Level 4 understanding of self, others, and the world around us.

The irony is that if we never attempt intentional growth, the catastrophic challenge is likely to come eventually through the loss of that loved one, which means the contradiction we will face will be the *ultimate* disconnection, dismissal, rejection, invalidation, or criticism. When that day comes, perhaps we will grow. But why wait for a catastrophe when the very people we are closest to, who occasionally take a little jab at our self-esteem, provide regular opportunities for us to lean into the challenge and grow to a place of greater intimacy, fulfillment, and understanding?

A rare handful of spouses and parents are able to make this transition to Level 5 without assistance, but not many. Most of us need a coach or some other intentional developmental relationship to help us talk through this new way of understanding ourselves and others. Our coaches need to help us get at *our* understanding and help us take responsibility for *our* side of the equation (our vulnerability) rather than helping us adapt our behavior so we don't have to face the vulnerability. Unless you can find a group to walk with you through this journey, this effort will most likely cost you time and money, but few things of great value are ever free.

I have met with a group of men almost every other Friday for the better part of the last decade. Our goal is to share challenges we are facing and to push each other to a more effective understanding of those challenges. The richest areas for growth most often arise around the topic of family—specifically, our relationships with spouses and children. We commit to do more than merely manage challenges. When we do the good work of pushing one another beyond Level 4, we create a space, through the questions we ask, to understand the vulnerability and values we don't even know we don't know. Family challenges most often drive movement toward Level 5, but we have also found topics of faith to have similar good results.

Faith

The Level 4 understanding of faith is necessarily self-authored and is the core underpinning to most everything else we hold to be true. Our beliefs about God, the afterlife, and human origins are foundational to our understanding of love, relationships, purpose, and how we know what we know. Until we eventually learn to hold these beliefs with an open hand—releasing our fearful grip on them—we will be unlikely to see the flaws in our Level 4 paradigm. We will be unable to take an objective view of our beliefs, which is required to move to Level 5. Therefore, opening ourselves to a more objective view of our faith will deepen that faith even as it deepens our understanding of everything else from a Level 5 perspective.

At Level 4 we can lean into faith challenges by examining our own and other faith ideologies more objectively, trusting that the values we have self-authored will become the grounding point for our evaluation of those different ideologies. This examination will create tension in what we have held to be true, and the tension will be the fuel for development to Level 5. If we take the perspective that most people are not crazy, are well intended, and have come to understand their own faith as the most reasonable answer to what they should base their lives on, then we can say to ourselves, *What they are saying makes sense to them. I just don't understand it yet.* Contrast this to our tendency to hear a different belief expressed and immediately think, *That doesn't make sense.*

This exploration can be done with deep-seated beliefs of all kinds—political, religious, denominational, etc. If you are Protestant, start by examining the Catholic perspective. Republicans can examine the Democratic position on key issues. Atheists and theists can trade views. You get the idea. The goal in all these cases is to begin to not only see a larger whole and find points of commonality, but even more to begin to take an objective view of the weakness and vulnerability of your own understanding. What makes this exercise so distinctive at Level 5 is that what we are finally letting go of are the self-authored beliefs (or faith) that we believed were the truest and best answers when we authored them as we became Level 4.

> One of the fundamental paradoxes of Level 5 is being a person of conviction while also being a person of curiosity. Can you be a leader that is more than your Level 4 convictions? Can you be open to having those values challenged in a way that deepens them? What happens when you and another person differ on principles? How do you remain open to new ideas and retain your strong convictions about what's right and what's wrong? Can you maintain a conversation long enough to hear what the person is really saying? Reconciling these tensions is the real work of leaders at Level 5.

Biases

A third challenge (closely related to the previous one) we can intentionally submit to is attempting to understand cultural differences in a way that pushes up against our deepest biases—personal tendencies toward one thing over another. They are deep-seated inclinations that influence the conclusions we make about almost everything. Some are known to us, but many are not—especially those formed in the context of the experiences that shape the Level 4 lens through which we see the world. Because many of them are so deep within our core that we are often unaware of their influence, they provide much potential to offer a new perspective on our Level 4 understanding—essentially a third-person, detached perspective. It is for this reason that intentionally creating exposure to the biases of others is such a powerful area for growth to Level 5.

Just as it was with beliefs and family, exploring the perspectives of those who have had a different cultural experience gets us to an "unknown place" in our own Level 4 understanding. If we think we don't have biases, that presumption is a pretty good indication of our Level 4 limitations, which provides a rich area for intentional accelerated growth.

The most pragmatic way to engage in this pursuit is through a reciprocal relationship with someone of a different race or culture. An open and honest dialogue characterized by mutually nonjudgmental explorations of the other's perspective opens the possibility of understanding ourselves in a new way. Our own perspectives become much clearer in contrast to the perspectives of others. This type of conversation can emerge only when both parties are totally committed to understanding the other without simultaneously defending their own understanding.

> "Men often hate each other because they fear each other; they fear each other because they don't know each other; they don't know each other because they can not communicate; they can not communicate because they are separated."
> —Martin Luther King, Jr., *Stride Toward Freedom*

I spent a couple of years in ongoing conversation with an African-American colleague I'll call Bill who was willing to walk this journey with me. We met once a month for eighteen months and talked for about two hours each time we met, using a few basic guidelines:

Do everything you can to put your personal perspective on the shelf when the other is talking;

Repeat what you hear the other say as closely as possible to his exact words;

Regularly ask, "Did I get that right or did I miss anything?" And if so, "Tell me more";

Stay focused and present in this way until there is no more—until he is finished; and

Switch sides and do the same steps above.

Through this reciprocal process it was surprising how many of our assumptions, previously unknown to us, emerged when contrasted with the assumptions of the other. This new understanding didn't happen overnight, but it occurred at an accelerated rate and took us beyond the well-honed paradigm of our Level 4 lenses because we were intentional.

The point of an exercise like this is not determining whose assumptions are more correct, but rather allowing the potential of a new understanding of our own biases to emerge. By openly and intentionally considering perspectives different from our own, we have the opportunity to see our perspectives in new ways that highlight previously hidden vulnerability.

It is very difficult to voluntarily submit to the challenge of other perspectives in the areas of beliefs, family, and biases. The common theme is that all of these challenges can eventually help you gain a much better perspective on what is unknown to your Level 4 lens. Most of us hold to our Level 4 understanding with a "fear grip" because it works so much better than the Level 3 perspective and protects our Level 4 system from coming apart. Our fear is that if we loosen our grip, something terrible might happen—we might fall out of love, we might lose our faith, we might not like what we find. However, if that grip is broken by much stronger circumstances of life, we may be forced into the same conclusions in the wake of the challenge. It takes real courage to let go intentionally.

The irony is that while releasing your grip feels like weakness, it actually increases your strength because it puts the underdeveloped muscles in your Level 4 system under stress. Eventually that stress will help ground your understanding in something bigger than itself. What will emerge is a profound set of values that can hold securely your Level 4 perspective much better than your grip ever could. Additionally, it holds your perspective, coordinated with others' differing perspectives, in an increasingly cohesive whole—one that is less threatened by the contrast of those differing perspectives to your own.

The challenges of family, beliefs, and biases are not the only ones that can contradict your Level 4 perspective in ways that lead to growth, but they can be applied almost universally to those who are fully Level 4 in their understanding.

One way to differentiate between Level 4 and Level 5 leaders is to think of their thought processes as a GPS system. For the Level 4 leaders, the system knows how to get them where they need to go. It can avoid the traffic jams, understand the value of shortcuts, and identify where the toll roads are. Level 5 leaders still have access to this GPS system, but what is different is that they are also interested in building new roads, and from Level 5 we realize that building those new roads will require the help of others. It takes years of experience to build a good GPS system and to have confidence that it will get you where you need to go. It takes courage to undertake the building of new roads. What if the new roads don't work as well or get us stuck? Risk is inherent in the life of the Level 5 Leader.

Motivating Growth Toward Level 5

Unlike all previous levels, the motivation to grow at Level 4 has to be self-imposed unless an unavoidable (and usually traumatic) challenge contradicts our Level 4 lens. This is why most people stop growing at Level 4. The longer our development is arrested there, the more intractable the Level 4 perspective will become. As I stated in earlier chapters, success and effectiveness at Level 4 may only increase this tendency to arrest growth because we have more influence and resources to resolve growth-producing challenges or make them go away.

If Level 4 individuals want to intentionally make progress toward Level 5, the primary motivator for growth must be an internal desire to grow based on the conclusion that the Map presented in this book is true and something better lies ahead. They must acknowledge that they are not done growing yet, that continued growth from this point forward will be more difficult than previous growth, and (barring some unavoidable and significant challenge) they will have to submit themselves to a process that allows them to begin to discover what they don't even know they don't know about themselves.

It's helpful for those committed to reaching Level 5 to intentionally create an enduring legacy. You will have a legacy whether you are intentional or not, but it's much better to have a say in it! Those who give forethought to their legacies tend to author decidedly Level 5 goals. Finishing well is an important consideration to those who are determined to keep growing to Level 5. The motivation to engage in the hard work of continued growth requires developing an internal motivation to be open, service-minded people others will actually seek out rather than avoid.

Those whose development arrests at Level 4 become at best benign older people who struggle with dissatisfaction over the constantly increasing irrelevancy of their understanding. At worst, they become cranky old people, angry at the changing world that contradicts their fixed Level 4 perspective, expressing themselves in ways that often alienate them from younger generations. We have all met people in both categories because the world has no shortage of individuals who stop growing after achieving success with an effective, self-authored, Level 4 understanding. If we don't see the value of moving on to Level 5, then we are most likely headed for the erroneous conclusion that "I've arrived," that my success is proof that I have done it well, and that I don't need any young whippersnappers to question my great wisdom.

In summary, growth is always motivated by the reconciliation of the tension between our current lens and the next lens on our journey. In the move from Level 4 to Level 5, that tension is the recognition that our current understanding must have inadequacies (weaknesses) that we can't see. This realization reveals that we are surely not done growing and that continued growth will demand of us a deeper understanding of the things we are trying to protect.

Accelerating Growth from Level 4 to Level 5

The most effective way to accelerate growth from Level 4 to Level 5 is by investing in the growth of others. As we saw in the challenges section above, we can ultimately only get a full perspective on our own perspective in contrast to differing perspectives. It is when we detach from our own perspective and truly invest in the growth of others that we can see something new about ourselves—something that we are unable to see through the lens of our Level 4 understanding. Great tragedy can accelerate growth, but only through investing in others can we begin to see our vulnerability at Level 4.

The challenge areas listed above and this notion of investing in the development of others are closely related. First of all, both relationship-oriented challenges (family and biases) are rich areas to explore because they have the potential to shine a light in the deep recesses of the assumptions that underpin our Level 4 awareness. Similarly, explorations of faith can be a rich area for growth because that which you put your trust in (faith) is so core to your understanding of everything else.

However, the intimidating work of tapping into the deepest parts of your identity isn't the only way to begin the journey from Level 4 to Level 5. You can also invest in the development of others who are not as far along the journey as you are—who don't have access to your inner core the same way that family, beliefs, and biases do. This group might include colleagues, friends, your friends' children, your kids' teachers or youth leaders, or even your bosses. As you first begin to get your developmental feet under you, it may be easier to invest in these relationships that are less threatening. You won't have to worry too much about their saying something that will provoke a defensive response, and it takes less emotional intensity to set your perspectives aside in order to be fully present in understanding them.

The biggest key in moving from Level 4 to Level 5, especially in terms of intentional development, is the need to focus all of your efforts on creating a new kind of openness and vulnerability. Moving from Level 4.0 to Level 4.2 requires you to acknowledge the incompleteness of the Level 4 system and values that you have self-authored. This early step is really about being open to the likelihood that your understanding is but one of many ways of making sense of the world. More than making a mere intellectual acknowledgment, you have to start seeing that others may have different effective ways to address situations than those that make sense to you at Level 4.

When two Level 4 leaders go after each other from positions based on strongly held principles and values, it can be a bloody, take-no-prisoners duel, and neither party is willing to budge. The best outcome you can hope for is that both finally relent and "agree to disagree." The problem with this settlement is that neither person learns and grows, and it doesn't improve the situation. They simply leave where they began.

In contrast, Level 5 leaders open their hands instead of clenching their fists, and they are willing to hear what the other person is saying. They ask, "Is there a third way to resolve the impasse? How can I be bigger and incorporate what the other is saying into my way of thinking?"

Quite often, both people in an argument have part of the truth (or a particular angle on the truth). If they can learn to listen to one another, they can find a mutually agreeable way to resolve the problem. The Level 5 leader is striving for commonality and wholeness.

Abraham Lincoln demonstrated what it looks like to recognize and honor the viability of differing perspectives. Toward the end of his second inaugural address, he said, "Neither party expected for the war, the magnitude, or the duration, which it has already attained. Neither anticipated that the *cause* of the conflict might cease with, or even before, the conflict itself should cease. Each looked for an easier triumph, and a result less fundamental and astounding. Both read the same Bible, and pray to the same God; and each invokes His aid against the other. It may seem strange that any men should dare to ask a just God's assistance in wringing their bread from the sweat of other men's faces; but let us judge not that we be not judged. The prayers of both could not be answered—that of neither has been answered fully."[41]

Lincoln was unwilling to condemn the perspective of his opponents even as he passed judgment on the "rightness" of it.

He concluded his speech by saying, "With malice toward none; with charity for all; with firmness in the right, as God gives us to see the right, let us strive on to finish the work we are in; to bind up the nation's wounds; to care for him who shall have borne the battle, and for his widow, and his orphan—to do all which may achieve and cherish a just, and a lasting peace, among ourselves, and with all nations."[42]

The Level 5 lens through which Lincoln understood himself, others, and the world acknowledged implicitly an awareness of his own limitations, vulnerabilities, and biases. He realized that "right" was determined by something bigger than himself; he knew his understanding was incomplete.

He saw that people on two different sides of a debate could "read the same Bible" and draw different conclusions. In Lincoln's address we see a humility combined with commitment and confidence. He recognized there were things he didn't know he didn't know. His speech also gives insight into his innate orientation toward understanding and investing in the needs of others. The effort to meet the needs of one's opponent results in values (peace and reconciliation) that are not only immediate, but also lasting.

Effective leaders see a lot of gray in life, but they help others define expectations and "the right thing" to do. What makes Level 5 leaders unique is *having strong standards* for their conduct and for others while simultaneously *being open* to having those values questioned. Can you be open enough to have your own standards questioned?

We can offer no magic bullet for accelerating development to Level 5. Each person who has reached Level 4 has arrived at a unique understanding by incorporating the outside sources of formative and early adult years into a self-authored, cohesive whole. Yet these unknown underpinnings must be identified and ultimately put at arm's length in order to objectively evaluate the weaknesses as well as the strengths of the understanding from which we make sense of ourselves, others, and the world.

Growth to Level 5 is no easy task. It cannot be achieved alone. It will take courage because it requires openness and vulnerability. It will take diligence because it is doesn't come naturally. Yet if continuous growth is our objective, we will never be fully satisfied until we eventually achieve the maturity of Level 5 and become able to influence others the way our heroes have influenced us.

Ask anyone who has pursued their Promised Land well . . . whatever it costs in terms of time, effort, and struggle, reaching your Promised Land is well worth it!

Consider This . . .

1. Has your Promised Land changed from what you named at the end of Chapter 1? If so, how would you define it at this point? Do you think it is an achievable destination? How close do you think you are to getting there?

2. Can you think of specific instances of people getting comfortable at Level 4 and arresting their growth rather than moving on to Level 5?

3. How about you: are you happy with your current rate of growth? If not, what do you think is slowing you down?

4. Presuming you are at Level 4, what steps are you willing to take to continue growing to Level 5:

    - Investing yourself in others? (If so, who comes to mind?)

    - Leaning into family challenges? (How, exactly?)

    - Leaning into faith challenges? (Where will you start?)

    - Leaning into bias challenges? (Who is someone with whom you can dialog?)

5. What do you want to be your legacy? In what way(s) does your response depend on developing Level 5 goals and values?

Chapter 12

LEVEL 5 . . . NOW WHAT?

Have you ever been away on a long trip, perhaps an extended family vacation (and maybe one with more than its fair share of bad weather, backseat squabbles, travel delays, and such)? After your lengthy time on the road, do you remember the feeling of driving into your hometown, and eventually into your own driveway? That sensation is approximately what it feels like to finally arrive at Level 5. Even though you've never been there before, it just feels right. It feels like home.

We get temporary tastes of that satisfying feeling of achievement along the way when we take on rigorous challenges that demand us to be at our best. Can I really hike to the top of that mountain . . . jump out of a plane . . . start a company . . . complete that novel . . . commit to that relationship . . . finish that marathon . . . get a graduate degree? When it's all over and done, we look back and revel in having completed something difficult and demanding—a challenge that might have beaten us, but didn't.

When you listen to older athletes discuss their glory days, do you ever hear them recall the games that were runaway victories? Not likely. What lasts in their memories are the hard-fought close calls. Last second buzzer beaters. Comebacks. Even devastating losses that were near-misses. (Don't you remember your close calls, too?)

Life at Level 5 provides a similar feeling of fulfillment, only more sustained. You have undergone series after series of challenges and contradictions, doing your best to deal with various difficulties through one lens after another, and then (finally!) it all makes sense. Perhaps this sounds like a fairytale to you—a "happily ever after" ending too good to be true. Yet you most likely know a rare few Level 5 people whose lives are proof positive of what is possible. Sit down and have coffee with one of them, and you will see that this is no fairytale. Getting to the end of the journey on your Map gives life a whole new meaning.

Those who arrive at Level 5 may seem like an exclusive club, but it doesn't have to be. Anyone can join who is willing to put in the effort to grow to that level. I hope you see the value in pursuing Level 5 as a Promised Land that will clarify your vision of yourself, others, and the world.

Growth at Level 5

Reaching Level 5, however, doesn't mean you're finished growing. It's just that by that point you stop using so much effort to address your own limitations, and you spend that energy instead for the benefit of others. Rather than wearing you down, as service tends to do whenever it is forced, your investment in others is what energizes you.

At Level 5 you have seen through the lenses of all the other levels, so it is only natural that you will empathize with people who are struggling through some of the same challenges that helped you get to where you are. You developed an ability to empathize with others back at Level 3, but only at Level 5 do you have the experience and insight to provide meaningful answers and advice. Not only that, but you know how to offer help at an appropriate level. Most likely you would approach your fourteen-year-old (Level 2) grandson quite differently than you would a Level 4 friend in a retirement home, even if both of them were suffering from loneliness.

One way to help others is to challenge them to reevaluate their priorities. At the earlier levels, many of us don't set good goals for ourselves. Once someone begins to understand the Map and the developmental growth process, everything becomes clearer. But far too many of us, rather than trying to arrive at self-awareness and more vulnerability, settle for much, much less.

When you come across a young executive determined to be a multimillionaire by the time he is thirty, you can ask some probing questions. Is it really wealth he is after, or contentment in life? Is she primarily interested in the acclaim of her peers, or does she want to make a real difference in the world?

When a Level 3 relative starts logging way too many hours on social media trying to build relationships by being "liked," you'll see an opportunity to step in as a trusted outside source. Who better to nudge her toward opportunities for IRL (in-real-life) community service and/or other challenges that will likely create contradictions in her understanding to perhaps move her a step closer to Level 4?

Level 5 leaders are very effective because they have learned the lessons of the previous levels, and they've successfully made the necessary transitions.[43] I once watched an executive address his staff. Within fifteen minutes he had addressed the challenges and opportunities of each level of leaders in the room. He didn't speak only to the Level 4 leaders. He detailed "what's in it for you" for all the Level 2 leaders, and he explained "here's how you see things from others' perspective" for Level 3 leaders. It was brilliant. He understood that everyone needed to follow him if he was going to lead a successful organizational change. He led his employees by meeting them where they were.

At Level 5 you are simultaneously achieving your bigger-me values and becoming more others-focused. Therefore, it will become hard *not* to see opportunities to help the people around you.

In return, your refreshing understanding of yourself, others, and the world will soon make you someone others want to emulate. Throughout this book I have cited examples of well-known Level 5 figures: Martin Luther King, Jr., Gandhi, Lincoln, Mother Teresa, and others. Their widespread influence is obvious. But just as impressive are "the unknowns" who live and serve at Level 5 who will never get their names in history books. They may be just as enlightened, just as conscientious, and just as service-oriented as those who become famous, but they simply have a smaller sphere of influence in which they operate.

If you haven't detected many of those people around, don't be too surprised. Individuals who thrive on service to others don't tend to call attention to themselves, although it often gets to the point where you can't help but notice how different they are.

At work, for instance, it doesn't take long to figure out which bosses are more "together" than most (and even less time to determine which ones aren't). You might expect to find a few Level 5 people in upper management, but don't stop there. If you look a little closer, you are likely to find some unassuming person at a lower level who does her job well and rarely gets special recognition. Yet you will notice coworkers continually streaming to her office for one reason or another. Some might want advice on a personal matter because she always seems to know just what to say. Others don't need advice; they simply want someone to listen for a moment. Still others realize that if they are having a bad day, they can stick their head in to say hello and leave a couple of minutes later feeling better. Human Resources managers ought to do more to identify Level 5 people in "regular jobs" and provide intentional opportunities for their influence (and perhaps compensation) because such people can often do more for performance effectiveness and even morale than a lot of costly programs and other options.

I was waiting for a coaching client outside his office when I overheard an executive assistant relating how sad she was that the executive she was serving had just been terminated. Her colleague was similarly distraught. She said there might not be another executive for her to serve, and so she might get fired too.

The first executive assistant answered, "Yes, that is true, but I choose to live in my faith and not in my fear." She was a woman who would not be defined by her circumstances. She could be sad and concerned, but she refused to give in to worry, helplessness, and hopelessness. Her faith wasn't a distant, abstract concept; it was very real, very present, and very comforting. She was Inside-Out, not Outside-In.

Too often we look to find Level 5s in the corner office, when in fact, we can often find them inhabiting the cubicle adjacent to the corner office.

Consider your religious community, if you have one. I don't want to get too detailed here because religion covers such a broad spectrum, but in faith communities it is often easy to discern which people are actually living into the standards of their faith and which ones aren't. Eastern religions are well known for their pursuit of enlightenment, where only a devoted few reach that goal. Judaism is faithful to the Torah and the high values detailed in the Law, the Prophets, and the Writings. In my own Christian tradition, much emphasis is placed on spiritual maturity—leaving behind old ways and seeking the higher values of love, joy, peace, and patience.

Enlightenment, high values, and maturity are all lifetime goals that, regardless of the religion, are talked about a lot more frequently than they are effectively modeled. But when you find people actually able to live out the teachings of their religion, they are certain to stand out. I might go so far as to say that it's useless to pursue spiritual maturity without also making the effort to grow Vertically. At Level 4 your understanding is better grounded and your practice is more authentic—at least you own it—yet if Vertical growth is arrested, a fixed Level 4 is not much more appealing than the shallower versions of Outside-In understanding. Spiritual maturity and developmental growth go hand in hand.

Home life is a considerably smaller venue than work or church, so it's usually much more obvious when Dad or Grandma grows to a Level 5 understanding. Previous chapters dealt with potential confusion that results when one spouse grows faster than the other and automatically expects the other to see life from a new perspective (most often when one of two Level 3 spouses grows to Level 4). Yet at Level 5 the person is able to detach from "my way" in order to meet others where they are. Effectiveness as a spouse and parent (or grandparent) improves as the person is able to encourage and promote growth of other family members at any other level.

Rare though they are, Level 5 individuals are out there in the workplace, in the faith community, and (I hope) in your family. It has long been my goal, and I hope it will become yours, to see such people become a lot more common in our regular circles of influence. Arrested growth at any level is wasted potential. Even worse, it is life less fulfilling than it could and should be.

Keep Persevering

Of course, while you are limited in how much you can do to help other people grow, you are totally in charge of your own continued growth. To that end, I want to leave you with some encouragement.

In Chapter 7 we looked at a formula for growth with three variables. Since then we have examined rather in-depth the Challenge and Contradiction component and how to decrease the Time factor by accelerating growth. As I close this book, I want to encourage your continued attention to the third aspect of growth: Perseverance.

Challenge and Contradiction

$$\frac{C + C}{T} \times P = VG$$

Vertical Growth

Perseverance

Time

Take another look at that formula of growth. How important is perseverance? It is the multiplicative function of mathematics and life. In middle school we learned that anything multiplied by zero equals zero. Therefore, when there is no perseverance, there is no elevated growth. We encourage our clients to see leadership as a muscle, and that muscle needs constant exercise to become strong.

When people have given up on the future, their enthusiasm, creativity, and tenacity wane. They no longer persevere, and they no longer use their leadership muscle—they neither grow nor lead.

If I haven't provided adequate inspiration for you, I hope you will look up quotes from astute observers throughout history who have noted the irreplaceable value of persisting and persevering through difficult times. Here are a few to get you started.

"Constant dripping hollows out a stone."

—*Lucretius, first-century Roman philosopher*

"Endure and persist; this pain will turn to your good by and by."

—*Ovid*

"Nothing in the world can take the place of persistence. Talent will not; nothing is more common than unsuccessful men with talent. Genius will not; unrewarded genius is almost a proverb. Education will not; the world is full of educated derelicts. Persistence and determination alone are omnipotent."

—*Calvin Coolidge*

"To travel hopefully is a better thing than to arrive, and the true success is to labor."

—*Robert Louis Stevenson*

"When you get in a tight place and everything goes against you till it seems as though you could not hold on a minute longer, never give up then, for that is just the time and the place the tide will turn."

—*Harriet Beecher Stowe*

"Let no feeling of discouragement prey upon you, and in the end you are sure to succeed."

—*Abraham Lincoln*

"Never give in, never give in, *never, never, never, never*—in nothing, great or small, large or petty—never give in except to convictions of honour and good sense."

—*Winston Churchill*

"You can eat an elephant one bite at a time."

—*Mary Kay Ash*

"In the game of life nothing is less important than the score at halftime."

—*Anonymous*

The importance of perseverance cannot be overestimated. Understanding the Map to developmental growth is relatively easy. I hope that by this point you have a decent comprehension of where you are, where you want to go, and how you can accelerate your growth. Yet when you put this book back on the shelf and return to the realities of life once more, you are certain to hit some new obstacles. When you do, lean into them.

My hope is that before too long you will be one of the first people who come to mind when your peers are asked about the most highly effective people they know. Ours can be an intensely competitive, affluent, petty, and ungrounded culture. You are bound to stand out if you are not only aware of, but also comfortable with, your weaknesses . . . if you are not overly sensitive to what others think about you . . . if you are confident in what you believe, yet are open to hearing other viewpoints. And as others see you as a more effective example, you continually experience more satisfaction with yourself and your circumstances.

Life is good in the Promised Land.

Consider This . . .

1. How do you think your life would be different at Level 5? (Consider challenges, use of time, relationships, values, priorities, etc.)

2. On a scale of 1 (least) to 10 (most), how would you rate your level of perseverance? Give some examples. How might you increase your number?

3. If you had a clearer understanding of yourself, the world, and others, who are some people you would like to help? What problems are they facing that seem to be overwhelming them at this point?

4. Who are some people with whom you can interact on a regular basis to help both of you continue to increase your effectiveness?

ENDNOTES

1 For specific examples, see Additional Resources: Eigel, 1998; Eigel & Kuhnert, 2005; Kuhnert & Lewis, 1987; Harris & Kuhnert, 2008; Strang & Kuhnert, 2009.

2 For specific examples, see Additional Resources: Kegan, 1994; Rooke & Torbert, 1998; Levinson, 1978; Burns, 1978; Maslow, 1971; Kegan & Lahey, 2009; Jaques, 1989; Kegan, 1994.

3 Robert Kegan, *The Evolving Self: Problem and Process in Human Development* (Cambridge, MA: Harvard University Press, 1982)

4 Kuhnert, K.W. & P. Lewis. 1987. Transactional and transformational leadership: A constructive developmental analysis. *Academy of management review*, 12(4), 648-657.

5 Dan Fogelberg, "The Higher You Climb," in *High Country Snows*, Epic Records, 1985.

6 What we want to do in this book is move thinking away from the traditional paradigm of the past fifty years of seeing leadership development as a complex function of traits, behaviors, and situations. What is new in this book is demonstrating how leaders grow and mature over the life course. Traits, behaviors, and situations are important but can only be understood in the context of the leaders' developmental trajectory. Where we are on that trajectory (what we are calling The Map) informs our traits, behaviors, and how we understand the contexts in which we lead. We don't see the world objectively, but rather see it through the subjectivity of our current developmental lens. The well-researched theory behind what we are doing is called constructive-developmental theory, and has historic roots in

the work of Jean Piaget (Jean Piaget & Barbel Inhelder, *The Growth of Logical Thinking from Childhood to Adolescence* [New York: Basic Books, 1958]); Lawrence Kohlberg (*Essays on Moral Development, Volume 2: The Psychology of Moral Development* [San Francisco: Harper and Row, 1984]); Robert Kegan (*The Evolving Self: Problem and Process in Human Development* [Cambridge, MA: Harvard University Press, 1982]); and Jane Loevenger [1983. On ego development and the structure of personality, *Developmental Review*, 3, 339-350]).

7   Koestenbaum, P. 2000. Do you have the will to lead? *Fast Company*, March, 223-230.

8   For excellent reviews of current knowledge about developing leaders, see Ellen Van Velsor, Cynthia D. McCauley, & Marian N. Ruderman (Eds.), *The Center for Creative Leadership Handbook of Leadership Development* (San Francisco: Jossey-Bass, 2010) and David V. Day, Michelle M. Harrison, & Stanley M. Halpin, *An Integrative Approach to Leader Development: Connecting Adult Development, Identity, and Expertise* (New York: Psychology Press, 2009).

9   John C. Maxwell, *The 21 Irrefutable Laws of Leadership* (Nashville: Thomas Nelson, 1998 and 2007).

10 See Bruce J. Avolio, *Leadership Development in Balance* (Mahwah, NJ: Lawrence Erlbaum, 2004).

11 We use these famous leaders as an example because of their tremendous courage and contributions to society. If we look, we'll find leaders at the highest levels of development all around us: teachers in our schools, leaders in our community, neighbors, and parents and grandparents. However, leaders at the highest developmental level don't necessarily hold positions of position or authority. It's a mistake to assume because someone has

accumulated wealth or status that he or she is a developmentally mature leader.

12 Robert Kegan, *In Over Our Heads: The Mental Demands of Modern Life* (Cambridge: Harvard University Press, 1994).

13 Robert Kegan & Lisa Laskow Lahey, *Immunity to Change* (Boston: Harvard Business Press, 2009).

14 See Cook-Greuter, S. R. 2004. Making the case for a developmental perspective. *Industrial and Commercial Training*, 36 (7), 275-281. Also Eigel, K.M. & Kuhnert, K.W. 2005. Authentic development: Leadership development level and executive effectiveness. *Monographs in Leadership and Management*, 3, 357-385.

15 Rooke, D. & Torbert, W.R. 1998. Organizational transformation as a function of CEOs' developmental stage. *Organization Development Journal*, 16(1), 11-28.

16 Ronald A. Heifetz, Alexander Grashow, and Marty Linsky, *The Practice of Adaptive Leadership: Tools and Tactics for Changing Your Organization and the World* (Boston: Harvard Business School Publishing, 2009).

17 Bethany Hamilton, *Soul Surfer* (New York: MTV Books/Pocket Books, 2006).

18 http://www.imdb.com/title/tt1596346/quotes

19 Stephen Duguid, *Can Prisons Work?* (Toronto: University of Toronto Press, 2000).

20 http://en.wikipedia.org/wiki/Tonya_Harding

21 Eigel, K.M. 1998. *Leader Effectiveness: A Constructive Developmental View and Investigation* (Doctoral dissertation, University of Georgia), 71-72.

22 Laurence J. Peter and Raymond Hull, *The Peter Principle: Why Things Always Go Wrong* (New York: HarperCollins, 1969, 2009).

23 Evert, C. 2010. Cleaning house, *Tennis*, 46(1).

24 Harvey, J.B. 1974, "The Abilene paradox: The management of agreement," *Organizational Dynamics* 3, 63–80.

25 Rosenthal, R. 1973. The Pygmalion effect lives. *Psychology Today*, September, 7, 4, 56-60, 62-63

26 Robert Kegan, from a presentation at Emory University, October 8, 1996.

27 Eigel, K.M. 1998. *Leader Effectiveness: A Constructive Developmental View and Investigation* (Doctoral dissertation, University of Georgia).

28 Robert Kegan, *The Evolving Self: Problem and Process in Human Development* (Cambridge, MA: Harvard University Press, 1982).

29 C.S. Lewis, *The Abolition of Man* (New York: Harper Collins, 1944), pp. 18-19.

30 Galinsky, E., Bond, J. T., Kim, S. S., Backon, L., Brownfield, E., & Sakai, K., *Overwork in America: When the way we work becomes too much, executive summary* (New York: Families and Work Institute, 2005).

31 Marcus Aurelius, *Meditations* (New York: Penguin, 2005).

32 Martin Luther King, Jr., *Letter From Birmingham Jail* (New York: HarperCollins, 1994).

33 Jim Collins, *Good to Great* (New York: HarperCollins, 2001).

34 Eigel, K.M. 1998. *Leader Effectiveness: A Constructive Developmental View and Investigation* (Doctoral dissertation, University of Georgia).

35 Robert Greenleaf, *Servant Leadership: A Journey into the Nature of Legitimate Power & Greatness* (Mahwah, NJ: Paulist Press, 1977, 1991, 2002), p. 27.

36 Cynthia D. McCauley and Christina A. Douglas, cited in *The Center for Creative Leadership Handbook of Leadership Development*, Cynthia D. McCauley, Russ S. Moxley, and Ellen Van Velsor (Eds.), (San Francisco: Jossey-Bass, 1998), pp. 160–193.

37 http://www.statista.com/statistics/278834/revenue-nike-adidas-puma-footwear-segment/

38 Robert Kegan and Lisa Lahey, *How the Way We Talk Can Change the Way We Work* (San Francisco: Jossey-Bass, 2002).

39 David Foster Wallace, Kenyon College Commencement Speech, May 21, 2005, web.ics.purdue.edu/~drkelly/DFWKenyonAddress2005.pdf

40 Robert Kegan, *In Over Our Heads: The Mental Demands of Modern Life* (Cambridge, MA: Harvard University Press, 1998).

41 Richard Beeman (series editor), *Lincoln Speeches* (New York: Penguin, 2012), p. 157.

42 Ibid., p. 158.

43 Barker, E.H. & Torbert, W.R. 2011. Generating and measuring practical differences in leadership performance at postconventional action-logics. In Angela H. Pfaffenberger, Paul W. Marko, & Allan Combs (Eds.), *The Postconventional Personality: Assessing, Researching, and Theorizing* (Albany: State University of New York Press, 2011), pp. 39-56.

ACKNOWLEDGEMENTS

So many people have helped us to come to this point. Some are nearby, some are far away, some are even in heaven. All of us have special ones who have loved us into being. Would you just take, along with us, ten seconds to think of the people who have helped you become who you are . . . those who have cared about you and wanted what was best for you in life. Ten seconds: we'll watch the time . . .

Whomever you have been thinking about, how pleased they must be to know the difference you feel they have made. You know they're the kind of people we do well to offer our world.

(This opening is adapted from Fred Rogers' acceptance speech when he received the 1997 Lifetime Achievement Award at the 24th annual Daytime Emmy Awards.)

We have pursued a field in which nothing is static. Leaders, their challenges, their understanding, and our own all continue to evolve. Even so, our understanding is possible because of those who preceded us in this field of work. While there are many philosophers, thinkers, and writers who have gone before, none has been more influential in our lives than Robert Kegan at Harvard. His 1982 book, *The Evolving Self,* as well as the work he did with Lisa Laskow Lahey in *How the Way We Talk Can Change the Way We Work,* has shaped and underpinned our understanding of adult development and has shaped the curriculum we created to challenge growth in others.

In pursuit of writing this book, even in the midst of leading groups of people through the structure and space for growth to happen at

The Leaders Lyceum and at the University of Georgia, we especially want to thank the team at Baxter Press: Pat Springle, Stan Campbell, and Anne McLaughlin. Your experience, insight, and pushing has brought a fifteen year effort to a conclusion. Thank you for your great work and for your persistence.

Bethany Phillips' help in fine-tuning the manuscript has been invaluable. We also want to thank our colleagues at The Leaders Lyceum who have helped shape the curriculum that has grown so many. We especially appreciate Dr. Sara Curtis, whose insights always lead to a clearer presentation.

I, Keith, want to acknowledge the influence, challenge, and support of my beautiful, smart, talented, and honest wife Leigh. You more than anyone have made this work I do possible. To Steve and Suzanne Eigel, my parents, and Tom and Alexandra Roddy, Leigh's parents, your unconditional love and support has enabled the work I am able to do, and therefore enabled whatever influence I have. To my Pescadores: John Fleming, Reed Haggard, Van Westmoreland, and Todd Williams; and to my dear friends Eric Zimmermann, Rocky Butler, and David McDaniel; all of you have pushed and propped me up in ways that have grown me. And to Karl, who for the last twenty-five years has been a teacher, colleague, sounding board and dear friend—thank you.

I, Karl, want to especially thank my beautiful and loving wife Gay and my children, Caroline and Belle, for your inspiration and encouragement. I love each of you to the moon and back. I want to also thank all the students in my classes who challenged me to explain myself more clearly. And to Keith, your friendship and humor keep the journey in perspective.

May all of your journeys be full and well-lived.

ADDITIONAL RESOURCES

We hope you have benefited from the principles in this book. If you would like to pursue additional insight into some of the specific topics, we are including this list of resources—many that we have based our research on, and some that we have written ourselves.

Avolio, B.J. 2007. Promoting more integrative strategies for leadership theory-building. *The American Psychologist,* 62, 25-33; discussion, 43-47.

Barker, E.H. and W.R. Torbert. 2011. Generating and measuring practical differences in leadership performance at postconventional action-logics. In Angela H. Pfaffenberger, Paul W. Marko, and Allan Combs (Eds.), *The Postconventional Personality: Assessing, Researching, and Theorizing* (Albany: State University of New York Press, 2011), pp. 39-56.

Basseches, M. 1989. Toward a constructive-developmental understanding of the dialectics of individuality and irrationality. In Deirdre A. Kramer and Michael J. Bopp (Eds.), *Transformation in Clinical and Developmental Psychology* (New York: Springer, 1989), pp. 188-209.

Baumeister, R.F. 1994. The crystallization of discontent in the process of major life change. In Todd F. Heatherton and Joel L. Weinberger (Eds.), *Can Personality Change?* (Washington, DC: American Psychological Association, 1994), pp. 281-297.

Blasi, A. 1998. Loevinger's theory of ego development and its relationship to the cognitive-developmental approach. In P. Michiel Westenberg, Augusto Blasi, and Lawrence D. Cohn (Eds.), *Personality Development: Theoretical, Empirical and Clinical Investigations of Loevinger's Conception of Ego Development* (Mahwah, NJ: Lawrence Erlbaum Associates Inc., 1998), pp. 13-26.

Brown, B. 2011. *Conscious leadership for sustainability: How leaders with a late-stage action logic design and engage in sustainability initiatives.* (Doctoral dissertation).

Cook-Greuter, S.R. 1999. *Postautonomous ego development: A study of its nature and measurement.* (Doctoral dissertation).

Cook-Greuter, S.R. 2004. Making the case for a developmental perspective. *Industrial and Commercial Training*, 36(7), 275-281.

Cook-Greuter, S.R. and Melvin E. Miller, *Transcendence and Mature Thought in Adulthood: The Further Reaches of Adult Development* (Lanham, MD: Rowman & Littlefield, 1994).

Day, D.V., 2011. Integrative perspectives on longitudinal investigations of leader development: From childhood through adulthood. *The Leadership Quarterly*, 22, 561-571.

Day, David V., Michelle M. Harrison, and Stanley M. Halpin, *An Integrative Approach to Leader Development: Connecting Adult Development, Identity, and Expertise* (New York: Psychology Press, 2009).

Drath, W.H., C.J. Palus, and J.B. McGuire. 2010. Developing interdependent leadership. In Ellen Van Velsor, Cynthia D. McCauley, and Marian N. Ruderman (Eds.), *The Center for Creative Leadership Handbook of Leadership Development*, 3rd Ed. (San Francisco: Jossey-Bass, 2010).

Eigel, K.M., *Leader Effectiveness: A Constructive-Developmental View and Investigation* (Athens, GA: University of Georgia, 1998).

Eigel, K.M. and K.W. Kuhnert, 2005. Authentic development: Leadership development level and executive effectiveness. *Monographs in Leadership and Management*, 3, 357-385.

Fisher, D. and W. Torbert. 1991. Transforming managerial practice: Beyond the achiever stage. *Research in Organizational Change and Development*, 5, 143-173.

Fowler, James W., *Stages of Faith: The Psychology of Human Development and the Quest for Meaning* (New York: Harper & Row, 1981).

Gilligan, Carol, *In a Different Voice: Psychological Theory and Women's Development* (Cambridge, MA: Harvard University Press, 1982).

Harris, L.S. and K.W. Kuhnert. 2008. Looking through the lens of leadership: A constructive development approach. *Leadership & Organization Development Journal*, 29(1), 47-67.

Heifetz, Ronald A., Alexander Grashow, and Marty Linsky, *The Practice of Adaptive Leadership: Tools and Tactics for Changing Your Organization and the World* (Boston: Harvard Business School Publishing, 2009).

Helsing, D., A. Howell, R. Kegan, and L. Lahey. 2008. Putting the "development" in professional development: Understanding and overturning educational leaders' immunities to change. *Harvard Educational Review*, 78, 437-465.

Helson, R. and B.W. Roberts. 1994. Ego development and personality change in adulthood. *Journal of Personality and Social Psychology*, 66, 911-920.

Jaques, Elliott, *Requisite Organization: The CEO's Guide to Creative Structure and Leadership* (Arlington, VA: Cason Hall & Co., 1989).

Joiner, Bill and Stephen Josephs, *Leadership Agility: Five Levels of Mastery for Anticipating and Initiating Change* (San Francisco: Jossey-Bass/Wiley, 2007).

Kegan, R. 1980. Making meaning: The constructive developmental approach to persons and practice. *The Personnel and Guidance Journal*, 58(5), 373-380.

Kegan, Robert, *The Evolving Self: Problem and Process in Human Development* (Cambridge, MA: Harvard University Press, 1982).

Kegan, Robert, *In Over Our Heads: The Mental Demands of Modern Life* (Cambridge, MA: Harvard University Press, 1994).

Kegan, Robert and Lisa Laskow Lahey, *How the Way We Talk Can Change the Way We Work: Seven Languages for Transformation* (San Francisco: Jossey-Bass/Wiley, 2001).

Kegan, Robert and Lisa Laskow Lahey, *Immunity to Change: How to Overcome It and Unlock the Potential in Yourself and Your Organization* (Boston: Harvard Business School Press, 2009).

Kegan, R., L. Lahey, and E. Souvaine. 1998. From taxonomy to ontogeny: Thoughts on Loevinger's theory in relation to subject-object psychology. In P. Michiel Westenberg, Augusto Blasi, and Lawrence D. Cohn (Eds.), *Personality Development: Theoretical, Empirical and Clinical Investigations of Loevinger's Conception of Ego Development* (Mahwah, NJ: Lawrence Erlbaum Associates, Inc., 1998), pp. 39-58.

Kohlberg, Lawrence, *The Psychology of Moral Development: Essays on Moral Development, Volume 2* (San Francisco: Harper & Row, 1984).

Kuhnert, K.W. 1994. Transforming leadership: Developing people through delegation. In Bernard M. Bass and Bruce J. Avolio (Eds.), *Improving Organizational Effectiveness through Transformational Leadership* (Thousand Oaks, CA: Sage Publications, 1994), pp. 10-25.

Kuhnert, K.W. and P. Lewis. 1987. Transactional and transformational leadership: A constructive developmental analysis. *Academy of Management Review*, 12(4), 648-657.

Laske, O.E. 2003. Executive development as adult development. In Jack Demick and Carrie Andreoletti (Eds.), *Handbook of Adult Development* (New York: Springer, 2003), pp. 565-584.

Levinson, Daniel J., *The Seasons of a Man's Life* (New York: Ballantine, 1978).

Lewis, P., G.B. Forsythe, P. Sweeney, P. Bartone, C. Bullis, and S. Snook. 2005. Identity development during the college years: Findings from the West Point longitudinal study. *Journal of College Student Development*, 46, 357-373.

Lewis, P. and T.O. Jacobs. 1992. Individual differences in strategic leadership capacity: A constructive/developmental view. In Robert L. Phillips and James G. Hunt (Eds.), *Strategic Leadership: A Multiorganizational-Level Perspective* (Westport, CT: Quorum Books, 1992), pp. 121-138.

Lucius, R.H., and K.W. Kuhnert. 1999. Adult development and the transformational leader. *The Journal of Leadership Studies*, 6, 78-85.

Manners, J. and K. Durkin. 2000. Processes involved in adult ego development: A conceptual framework. *Developmental Review*, 20, 475-513.

Manners, J., K. Durkin, and A. Nesdale. 2004. Promoting advanced ego development among adults. *Journal of Adult Development,* 11(1), 19-27.

Maslow, Abraham H., *The Farther Reaches of Human Nature* (New York: Viking, 1971).

McCauley, C.D., W.H. Drath, C.J. Palus, P.M.G. O'Connor, and B.A. Baker. 2006. The use of constructive-developmental theory to advance the understanding of leadership.

The Leadership Quarterly, 17, 634-653.

Merriam, S.B. and M.C. Clark. 2006. Learning and development: The connection in adulthood. In Carol Hoare (Ed.), *Handbook of Adult Development and Learning* (New York: Oxford University Press, 2006), pp. 27-51.

Merron, K.A. (1985). *The relationship between ego development and managerial effectiveness under conditions of high uncertainty.* (Doctoral dissertation).

Merron, K.A., D. Fisher, and W. Torbert. 1987. Meaning making and management action. *Group and Organization Studies,* 12(3), 274-286.

Miller, M. (1994). World views, ego development, and epistemological changes from the conventional to the postformal: A longitudinal perspective. In Melvin E. Miller and Susanne R. Cook-Greuter (Eds.), *Transcendence and Mature Thought in Adulthood: The Further Reaches of Adult Development* (Lanham, MD: Rowman & Littlefield Publishers, 1994), pp. 147-178.

Miller, M.E. and S.R. Cook-Greuter. 1994. From postconventional development to transcendence: Visions and theories. In Melvin E. Miller and Susanne R. Cook-Greuter (Eds.), *Transcendence and Mature Thought in Adulthood: The Further Reaches of Adult*

Development (Lanham, MD: Rowman & Littlefield Publishers, 1994), pp. xv-xxxii.

Palus, Charles J. and Wilfred H. Drath, *Evolving Leaders: A Model for Promoting Leadership Development in Programs* (Greensboro, NC: Center for Creative Leadership, 1995).

Piaget, Jean and Barbel Inhelder (Trans. Anne Parsons and Stanley Milgram), *The Growth of Logical Thinking: From Childhood to Adolescence* (New York: Basic Books, 1958).

Rooke, D. and W.R. Torbert. 1998. Organizational transformation as a function of CEOs' developmental stage. *Organization Development Journal*, 16(1), 11-28.

Reams, J. 2002. *The consciousness of transpersonal leadership.* (Doctoral Dissertation)

Reams, J. 2005. What's integral about leadership? *Integral Review.* 1, 118-132.

Russell, C.J. and K.W. Kuhnert. 1992. Integrating skill acquisition and perspective taking capacity in the development of leaders. *Leadership Quarterly: An International Journal of Political, Social and Behavioral Science,* 3, 335-353.

Russell, C. and K.W. Kuhnert. 1992. New frontiers in management selection systems: Where measurement technologies and theory collide. *Leadership Quarterly: An International Journal of Political, Social and Behavioral Science,* 3, 109-135.

Snarey, J., L. Kohlberg, and G. Noam. 1983. Ego development in perspective: Structural stage, functional phase, and cultural age-period models. *Developmental Review,* 3(3), 303-338.

Steeves, R.A. 1997. Why leaders are effective: an examination into leader developmental level and leader-follower developmental fit as predictors of effective leadership. *Dissertation Abstracts International,* 58, 02A.

Strang, S.E. and K.W. Kuhnert. 2009. Personality and leadership developmental levels as predictors of leader performance. *The Leadership Quarterly,* 20, 421-433.

Torbert, Bill, Susanne Cook-Greuter, Dalmar Fisher, Erica Foldy, Alain Gauthier, Jackie Keeley, David Rooke, Sara Ross, Catherine Royce, Jenny Rudolph, Steve Taylor, and Mariana Tran, *Action Inquiry: The Secret of Timely and Transforming Leadership* (San Francisco: Berrett-Koehler Publishers, 2004).

Torbert, William R., *The Power of Balance: Transforming Self, Society, and Scientific Inquiry* (Newbury Park, CA: Sage, 1991).

Torbert, W.R. (1994). Cultivating postformal adult development: Higher stages and contrasting interventions. In Melvin E. Miller and Susanne R. Cook-Greuter (Eds.), *Transcendence and Mature Thought in Adulthood: The Further Reaches of Adult Development* (Lanham, MD: Rowman & Littlefield Publishers, 1994), pp. 181-204.

Valcea, S., M.R. Hamdani, M.R. Buckley, and M.M. Novicevic. 2011. Exploring the development potential of leader–follower inter-actions: A constructive-developmental approach. *The Leadership Quarterly,* 22(4), 604-615.

Van Velsor, E., and W.H. Drath. 2004. A lifelong developmental per-spective on leader development. In Cynthia D. McCauley and Ellen Van Velsor (Eds.), *The Center for Creative Leadership Handbook of Leadership Development, Second Edition* (San Francisco: Jossey-Bass, 2004), pp. 383-414.

Vincent, N., L. Ward, and L. Denson. 2013. Personality preferences and their relationship to ego development in Australian leadership program participants. *Journal of Adult Development,* 20(4), 197-211.

Vincent, N., L. Ward, and L. Denson. 2015. Promoting post-conventional consciousness in leaders: Australian community leadership programs. *The Leadership Quarterly, 26,* Issue 2: 238–253.

Wilber, Ken, *Integral Psychology: Consciousness, Spirit, Psychology, Therapy* (Boston: Shambhala Publications, 2000).

Zaccaro, Stephan J., *The Nature of Executive Leadership: A Conceptual and Empirical Analysis of Success* (Washington DC: American Psychological Association, 2001).

ABOUT THE AUTHORS

For the past twenty-five years, Keith Eigel has been focused on growing leaders across corporate, nonprofit, ministry, family, and educational settings. He cofounded and heads up the team at The Leaders Lyceum, an organization dedicated to facilitating the growth of executive and next generation leaders. Keith received his Masters and Doctorate in Industrial and Organizational Psychology at the University of Georgia. He and his wife Leigh headquarter their varying influence with their four children from their Atlanta, Georgia home.

Karl Kuhnert has dedicated his entire adult life to understanding great leadership. On the faculty at the University of Georgia since 1987, he chaired the Industrial/Organizational Psychology Program for eight years and has been recognized as the Undergraduate Teacher of the Year four times. Karl received his Doctorate from Kansas State University, but still has a special place in his heart for Penn State where on scholarship he played football and learned the values of education and resoluteness. Karl and his wife Gay live with their two daughters in Athens, Georgia.

The
LEADERS LYCEUM

In 1996, Karl and I presented a curriculum experience for a group of faculty at the University of Georgia. We hoped we could facilitate the kind of transformational development that we had seen in effective one-to-one coaching relationships—an expensive process that is usually limited to only the top positions in most organizations. Our goal was to make affordable this same kind of transformational development by scaling it to a group level so it could be pushed down to the upcoming generations of leaders whose influence is real, but who often feel stuck or in over their heads. That original curriculum, through much trial and error and over the ensuing decade, became the underpinning of the work we do at The Leaders Lyceum—an Atlanta-based organization serving corporate, nonprofit, and educational leaders in their pursuit of the kind of influence they hope to have.

The Leaders Lyceum strives to help all leaders identify and leverage their real-time/real-world challenges and then create the space, structure, and teaching that allows those challenges to fuel the kind of growth we have presented in this book—growth that can lead to greater effectiveness in leadership, life, and legacy.

For more information on The Leaders Lyceum and our leader development offerings, go to www.LeadersLyceum.com. In addition to general information, you will find a number of helps specific to this book, including the complete interviews with Stan (Chapter 3), Joe (Chapter 4), Kate (Chapter 5), and Henry (Chapter 6); samples of the Growth Gap Tool and GO Statements (Chapter 8); helpful articles; downloadable tools; and how to order additional copies of this book.

TO ORDER MORE COPIES

To order more copies of this book, go to

www.LeadersLyceum.com